ESSENTIAL
TURKEY WEST COAST

Original text by Sean Sheehan
Updated by Lindsay Bennett

© AA Media Limited 2009
First published 2009. Reprinted August 2009.

ISBN: 978-0-7495-5982-3

Published by AA Publishing, a trading name of AA Media Limited, whose registered
office is Fanum House, Basing View, Basingstoke, Hampshire RG21 4EA. Registered
number 06112600.

AA Media Limited retains the copyright in the original edition © 1999 and in all
subsequent editions, reprints and amendments

A CIP catalogue record for this book is available from the British Library

Colour separation: MRM Graphics Ltd
Printed and bound in Italy by Printer Trento S.r.l.

A04173
Maps in this title produced from map data © New Holland Publishing (South Africa)
(Pty) Ltd, 2007

About this book

This book is divided into five sections.

The essence of Turkey west coast
pages 6–19
Introduction; Features; Food and drink;
Short break including the 10 Essentials

Planning pages 20–33
Before you go; Getting there; Getting
around; Being there

Best places to see pages 34–55
The unmissable highlights of any visit
to Turkey's west coast

Best things to do pages 56–73
Great places to have lunch; top
activities; stunning views; places to
take the children; best Turkish baths
and massage and more

Exploring pages 74–185
The best places to visit along Turkey's
west coast, organized by area

Maps

All map references are to the maps on
the covers. For example, Bodrum Kalesi
has the reference ➕ K16 – indicating
the grid square in which it is to be found

Admission prices

Inexpensive (under YTL5);
Moderate (YTL5–YTL10);
Expensive (over YTL10)

Hotel prices

Prices are per room per night:
£ budget (under YTL150);
££ moderate (YTL150–YTL250);
£££ expensive (over YTL250)

Restaurant prices

Prices are for a three-course meal per
person without drinks:
£ budget (under YTL20);
££ moderate (YTL20–YTL40);
£££ expensive (over YTL40)

Contents

BEST THINGS TO DO

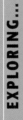

EXPLORING...

The essence of...

Western Turkey is steeped in 5,000 years of dramatic history, and is intoxicating for anyone with an interest in the origins of European civilization. It started here – not in Athens or Rome – when Greek colonists sailed across the Aegean to the coast of modern-day Turkey and established settlements that would nurture the first-known historians, geographers, philosophers and poets. Many inspiring ruins of this cradle of European culture still stand, alongside resort hotels, sandy beaches, watersports facilities, and discos that belt out the latest sounds as the sun rises over Homer's Troy.

features

Beaches lapped by turquoise water, rocky crags carpeted with pine trees that look down on olive groves, blue and white beehives set out on bare rocks, sunseekers relaxing on white sand beaches, antique fishing villages and ancient civilizations – the images of Turkey in the travel brochures are based on fact, and they only hint at the richness of the Aegean coast. The major resorts are Kuşadası, Bodrum and Marmaris, with Fethiye and Ölüdeniz not far behind. Turkish people are convivial and curious, homely and hospitable to a fault, and for many visitors the lasting impression they have of the country is not the food, the beaches or the ancient sites, but of the straightforward friendliness of the people they have met.

Few destinations can match western Turkey's capacity to fulfil the disparate needs of so many different kinds of visitors. If you want to dance and party till 5am and sleep in until the late afternoon, then Bodrum and other resorts are waiting to receive you. If Greek and Roman art is more to your liking, then Ephesus is just one of the many incredibly well-preserved sites waiting to be explored. Best of all, do both and find time for everything else in between.

GEOGRAPHY

● Turkey's west coast stretches south from Çanakkale to merge with the Mediterranean off Patara, some 500km (310 miles) south as the crow flies. The waters of the Çanakkale Boğazi (Dardanelles; ➤ 85) are a traditional dividing line between Europe and Asia, which makes most of western Turkey a part of Asia. Until quite recently, it was generally referred to as 'Asia Minor'.

PEOPLE

● The population of western Turkey is remarkably homogeneous. Nearly everyone is technically ethnically Turkish, and the non-Muslim proportion of the population is just around 1 per cent.

RELIGION

● Virtually everyone is a Muslim, and mosques are commonplace, but the secular aspect of Turkish society is more obvious along the western Turkish coast than anywhere else in Turkey.

● Elsewhere in Turkey, the month-long religious festival of Ramadan (➤ 24) transforms daily life, but holidaymakers on the western Aegean coast may not even notice it is happening. Western dress and manners are commonplace.

food & drink

Turkish cuisine has been open to various influences, a legacy of the far-reaching Ottoman Empire, but the underlying characteristic is a determination to conserve the natural tastes of fresh ingredients. The country imports very little food: meat, fruit and vegetables, honey and jam are all produced in Turkey.

WHAT TO EAT

Breakfast usually consists of bread, honey, sheep's cheese and olives, served with tea. Depending on the class of hotel, a more substantial English or American breakfast may receive token acknowledgement in the form of cereals, cooked eggs and ham. Lunch is also a relatively light affair, with the evening meal being the main meal of the day.

   Traditional starters take the form of delicious hot and cold *meze* – small dishes using a variety of ingredients, for example

puréed aubergines *(patlıcan salatasi)*, stuffed vine leaves *(zeytinagli yaprak dolmasi)*, and finely rolled cheese pastries *(sigara böreği)*. Main dishes are usually based around lamb or beef, although boiled chicken *(tavuk)* and roast chicken *(pilav)* are also popular. Restaurants usually have fresh fish on the menu, such as turbot, bream, sea bass, mussels and crab. Sweet desserts are highly appreciated in Turkey, and can be glorious: *baklava* (puff pastry with syrup and nuts), custard-based desserts and rice puddings are all favourites.

RESTAURANTS

There are two main types of restaurant: the plain *lokanta* and the more formal *restoran*. The *lokanta* keeps its warm, previously cooked, dishes on display in steamtrays. The fare is simple but filling, usually consisting of stews, stuffed peppers, beans and rice. A *restoran* should offer a range of courses (soup, *meze*, meat dishes and desserts) and, unlike the average *lokanta*, will serve beer and wine. There are also specialist restaurants, the names of which will indicate their speciality. The *pide salonu*, or *pideci*, offers pitta bread with various fillings, the *köftesi* serves meatballs, and the *kebapçı* concentrates on roast meat.

BREAD

White bread is ubiquitous – it is served with breakfast, lunch and dinner. When fresh it is soft and palatable, but it soon becomes stale. Brown bread is difficult to find in the coastal resorts, but it does exist and is worth seeking out in bakeries.

SOMETHING TO DRINK?

Tea *(çay)* is drunk throughout the day, served in tiny, gold-rimmed glasses and without milk. Apple tea *(elma çay)* is a particular favourite with the proprietors of carpet shops

who wish to make potential customers feel welcome. Turkish coffee is not as common as you might expect, although Turkish people do drink it in various degrees of sweetness *(sade* is without sugar, *az* and *orta* are medium, while *çok* is saturated in sugar).

The national alcohol is *raki*, distilled from grape juice and flavoured with aniseed, but Turkish wine is widely available in shops and licensed restaurants. The less expensive brands will not suit everyone's palate. Locally brewed beer *(bira)* is readily available, and the Efes brand is popular with both locals and visitors. Domestically produced gin *(cin)*, vodka *(vokta)* and cognac *(kanyak)* are less expensive than imported products but, other than in cocktails, the difference in taste is significant.

short break

If you have only a short time to visit Turkey's west coast and would like to take home some unforgettable memories, you can do something local and capture the real flavour of the region. The following suggestions are a range of sights and experiences that won't take very long, won't cost very much and will make your visit special.

● **Visit Efes (Ephesus),** Rome's renowned Asian capital, where a quarter of a million citizens once lived. It is one of the world's best-preserved ancient cities (➤ 42–43).

● **Venture into a** *hamam* (Turkish bath) and experience the bath of a lifetime, followed by an invigorating massage on the stone platform built over the oven that heats the water.

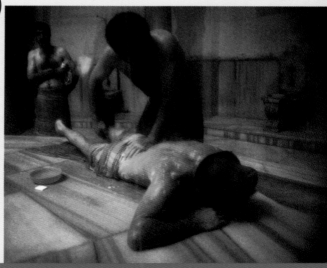

- **Explore one of the ancient Greek or Roman theatres,** many of which are remarkably well preserved, built from stone into the hillside (➤ 42–43, 54–55, 112).

- **Relax and talk in the street** with Turkish people, perhaps over a glass of tea or a game of backgammon, and discover their friendliness and sense of hospitality.

- **Enjoy a selection of Turkish *meze*** (appetizers, ➤ 12–13) with fresh bread, accompanied by a glass of *raki* (➤ 15), the national alcoholic drink.

● **Go shopping in a bazaar** and be prepared to get lost. The bazaar in İzmir (Smyrna) is especially labyrinthine (➤ 69).

● **Party till dawn** at Bodrum's Halikarnas Disco (➤ 148) or one of the many other nightspots.

● **Watch the sun set over Çanakkale Boğazi (the Dardanelles),** the narrow strait that separates Asia from Europe and has inspired lovers, poets and generals, often with tragic consequences (➤ 85).

● **Cruise the Aegean,** if only for a day, from Bodrum, Marmaris or Fethiye, in a traditional *gület*. Bathe on an otherwise inaccessible beach and swim in the crystal-clear waters (► 136).

● **Go snorkelling or scuba diving**: Bodrum, Kuşadası and Marmaris are all good centres for both.

Planning

Before you go

WHEN TO GO

JAN	FEB	MAR	APR	MAY	JUN	JUL	AUG	SEP	OCT	NOV	DEC
13°C	14°C	17°C	21°C	25°C	30°C	34°C	34°C	31°C	26°C	19°C	14°C
55°F	57°F	63°F	70°F	77°F	86°F	93°F	93°F	88°F	79°F	66°F	57°F

🌥 High season   🌥 Low season

The climate on the western coast of Turkey is typically Mediterranean, with over 300 days of sunshine a year and low rainfall in the summer months. The best months to visit are May, June and September, when temperatures are comfortable and the crowds not too dense. In July and August, temperatures rise into the 30s°C (80s/90s°F), making sightseeing uncomfortable. The crowds of holidaymakers at this time also mean the beaches, hotels and restaurants are full. Winters are generally mild, though a cold wind can blow down the Aegean Sea from the northeast making it feel chilly. Many hotels and restaurants in the coastal resorts close between October and late April, which limits eating and staying options. However, tourist numbers drop dramatically, which means you will be able to explore the ancient sites without having to fight the crowds.

WHAT YOU NEED

		UK	Germany	USA	Netherlands	Spain
●	Required					
○	Suggested					
▲	Not required					

All visitors require a passport with at least six months beyond the date of entry. If you have Turkish nationality, a Turkish ID card will suffice.

	UK	Germany	USA	Netherlands	Spain
Passport (or National Identity Card where applicable)	●	●	●	●	●
Visa (obtainable on arrival – check regulations before your journey)	●	▲	●	●	●
Onward or Return Ticket	○	○	○	○	○
Health Inoculations	▲	▲	▲	▲	▲
Health Documentation (Health Insurance, ➤ 23)	▲	▲	▲	▲	▲
Travel Insurance	○	○	○	○	○
Driving Licence (EU or national)	●	●	●	●	●
Car Insurance Certificate (if own car)	●	●	●	●	●
Car Registration Document (if own car)	●	●	●	●	●

WEBSITES

www.gototurkey.co.uk
www.tourismturkey.org

www.kultur.gov.tr/en

TOURIST OFFICES AT HOME

In the UK

Turkish Culture and Tourism Office
Fourth Floor
29–30 St James's Street
London SW1A 1HB
☎ 020 7838 7778;
Fax: 020 7925 1388;
www.gototurkey.co.uk

In the US

Turkish Information Office
821 United Nations Plaza

New York, NY 10017
☎ 212/687-2194;
Fax: 212/599-7568;
www.tourismturkey.com

2525 Massachusetts Avenue NW
Washington DC 20008
☎ 202/612-6800;
Fax: 202/319-7446;
(this office also deals with enquiries
from Canada)

HEALTH INSURANCE

Arrange travel insurance in your home country before arriving in Turkey.
Turkey is not a member of the EU, so EU visitors cannot obtain free
medical treatment. Where there are reciprocal agreements you generally
need to pay first then get reimbursed.

Dental treatment must be paid for. Check your travel insurance to see
whether, and to what extent, dental treatment is covered.

TIME DIFFERENCES

| GMT | Turkey | Germany | USA (NY) | Netherlands | Spain |
| 12 noon | 2PM | 1PM | 7AM | 1PM | 1PM |

Local time is 2 hours ahead of Greenwich Mean Time (GMT+2),
but daylight saving (GMT+3) operates between late March and
late September.

NATIONAL HOLIDAYS

1 Jan *New Year's Day*

23 Apr *Independence Day*

19 May *Atatürk Commemoration Youth and Sports Day*

30 Aug *Commemoration of the Turkish victory over the Greeks in 1922*

29 Oct *Commemoration of the Proclamation of the Republic in 1923*

Moveable holidays
Islamic holidays, the dates of which change from year to year, are also recognized in most of Turkey.

WHAT'S ON WHEN

Religious holidays and festivals

Only a few special days occur at the same time every year in Turkey because they are calculated according to the Muslim lunar calendar. *Kurban Bayramı* is a festival of sacrifice commemorating Abraham's willingness to sacrifice his son Isaac. It is marked by the sacrifice of millions of lambs across the country and the distribution of the meat to those in need. During the month of Ramadan (starting 25 October in 2003), Muslims do not eat, drink or smoke between sunrise and sunset,

but this should not cause a problem for anyone travelling along the Aegean coast. The end of Ramadan is celebrated by a festival *(Şeker Bayramı)*, marked by family get-togethers and the exchanging of sweets.

Local events

Mid-Jan to late Feb is the time to watch for camel-wrestling in the Selçuk and Denizli areas.

15 Mar in Çanakkale is usually marked by special events, commemorating the 1915 victory at sea.

Mid-May is the Marmaris Maritime and Spring Festival in Marmaris when regatta and arts events take place. There is also a yacht race during the first week of November.

The second half of May brings a Jazz Festival to Bodrum (tel: 0252 316 7718).

Mid-Jun to early Jul is the time of the International İzmir Festival, with events also taking place at Selçuk and Ephesus.

In **early Jun** Pamukkale holds a festival in the amphitheatre of ancient Hieropolis.

Jul and Aug see Çeşme host a Song and Music competition.

In **Aug/Sep,** İzmir hosting its annual International Trade Fair. The practical result of this for non-commercial visitors is that the better hotels, and even restaurants, will be heavily booked.

Early Sep is the Selçuk Festival, featuring Turkish folk dances and musical events.

Nov is the second of the two Marmaris International Yacht Race weeks. İzmir also hosts the İzmir International Short Film Festival (tel: 0232 482 0498) for productions in many languages.

Market days

It is always worth asking at the local tourist office about where and when the weekly market is held. Such market days are important to Turkish people living in the countryside, and the local town will be visibly busier with the influx. Usually there will be an area in town set apart for stalls and, although the merchandise is not targeted at tourists, the scene is still a lively one and worth a visit. Kuşadası is an exception in that the two weekly markets (Tuesday and Friday) are also aimed at tourists. You can get more information at local tourist offices.

Getting there

BY AIR

Adnan Menderes Airport

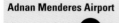

25km (16 miles) to İzmir

🚋 N/A

🚌 30 minutes

🚗 20 minutes

Milas-Bodrum Airport

50km (31 miles) to Bodrum

🚋 N/A

🚌 40 minutes

🚗 50 minutes

Turkish Airlines has scheduled flights to İzmir via Istanbul from major European cities, and onwards to all domestic airports in Turkey including İzmir, Dalaman and Bodrum. During the tourist season direct charter flights fly to resort areas.

Visitors arriving from Britain have to pay a visa fee (£10 per person) on entry at the airport. Visitors from the Republic of Ireland pay 10 euros.

Adnan Menderes Airport at İzmir (tel: 0232 455 0000; www.adnanmenderesairport.com) is the major airport hub for this coast, but there are few direct scheduled flights from the UK. Turkish Airlines flies direct to London, Manchester and Dublin and British Airways flies direct from London. Most scheduled flights are via Istanbul with Turkish Airlines, or various German cities with Lufthansa. Charter flights to Adnan Menderes feed Çeşme, Foça and the north of the region.

Milas-Bodrum Airport (tel: 0252 523 0080; www.bodrum-airport.com) serves the bulk of the resort towns of the Turkish west coast from Bodrum in the south to Kuşadası in the north. Scheduled flights arrive via Istanbul or via several German cities, with the bulk of flights from the UK being charter flights provided by the major package holiday companies. These run from late April to mid-October only.

Dalaman Airport (tel: 0252 792 5555; www.atmairport.aero) serves the very southern section of the West Coast with year-round scheduled flights from other Turkish towns and cities, and charter flights from 20 airports in the UK, feeding the Marmaris Peninsula and Fethiye between late April and mid October.

BY RAIL

The legendary Orient Express train linked London to Istanbul, and less luxurious services still link the two cities daily via Bucharest, Sofia or Athens, with the journey taking three or four days. From Istanbul there are services with Türkiye Cumhuryeti Devlet Demiryollan (TCDD), Turkish National Railways (www.tcdd.gov.tr) to Bandırma and then from Bandırma to İzmir for onward connection to the resorts and attractions.

BY BOAT

The west coast of Turkey is connected to various Greek Aegean islands by ferry, including Chios, Kos, Lésvos, Rhodes and Sámos, During the summer these ferries run daily or almost daily while between October and April services may drop in frequency. Çeşme/İzmir is linked by car ferry to the Italian ports of Ancona and Brindisi, with a service by RECA Marmara Sea Lines (tel: 0232 712 2223; www.marmaralines.com). These run from April to October with one service per week, journey time 42 to 57 hours.

BY CAR

You can drive through Europe to Turkey, either across northern Italy and the states of the former Yugoslavia or to Brindisi or Ancona to take the ferry across the Mediterranean (see above). Journey time is around four days from London. From northern Turkey, the easiest land route is down the Gelibolu peninsula, crossing the Dardanelles by ferry (15 minutes) at Çanakkale and following the main 550 route south via Troy, Ayvalık and Pergamum to the southern part of the coast. If you want to skip the long road routes, there's an Istanbul/Bodrum car ferry run by Denizline (www.denizline.com) from May to September, taking 22 hours.

BY BUS

Ulusoy bus company (tel: 0252 444 1888; www.ulusoy.com.tr) runs the Eurolines (www.eurolines.com) service for Turkey, connecting to services into Europe via northern Greece.

Getting around

PUBLIC TRANSPORT

Internal flights Turkish Airlines (tel: 0212 444 0849; www.thy.com) operate domestic flights connecting Istanbul, Ankara and most of Turkey's major cities with the airports at Dalaman, İzmir and Bodrum. Onur Air (tel: 0212 663 2300; www.onurair.com.tr), Atlasjet Airlines (tel: 0216 444 3387; www.atlasjet.com) and Fly Air (tel: 444 4359 within Turkey; www.flyair.com.tr) operate low-cost flights between main Turkish hubs.

Trains There is a very limited, and usually very slow, train service covering a small area of western Turkey, and few visitors use it. From İzmir, trains run to Selçuk, Denizli and Manisa. For reservations tel: 444 8233 (national number) for information; www.tcdd.gov.tr.

Buses Buses are the most popular and practical means of getting around. The service is usually very reliable and professional, with air-conditioning and refreshment and entertainment facilities on board. Tickets can be purchased at the bus station *(otogar)*, in advance, and usually on the bus, if you board after the starting point. Smoking is not allowed on buses.

Boat trips The best way to see the coastline, and to reach otherwise inaccessible coves, is by boat. In all the major resorts, boat operators will be found at the harbour. Longer cruises with a crew, lasting between three and seven days, are especially popular from Bodrum and Marmaris. Ferries to Greek islands are commonplace.

***Dolmuş*/minibus** A *dolmuş* is a shared taxi. You pay according to the distance travelled and can get on or off anywhere along the route. For most travel, the *dolmu*ş is a minibus and you pay on board. For local travel between villages or small towns it is the best means of transport.

TAXIS

Taxis are usually yellow, and can be hailed from the street or from ranks in the major resorts. Fares may be metered, but it's best to agree on a price beforehand. Fares double between midnight and 6am.

FARES AND CONCESSIONS

Most sights offer discounts for children. Holders of an International Student Identity Card (ISIC) may be able to obtain some concessions on travel and entrance fees, and passengers with disabilities get a substantial discount on trains. There is the occasional hostel where an ISIC card is helpful. Inexpensive accommodation is also available in pensions (*pansiyons*).

On the whole, concessions are few and far between and apply only to Turkish citizens.

DRIVING

- Drive on the right.
- Speed limit on motorways: 120kph/74.4mph.
- Speed limit in open areas: 90kph/55.8mph.
- Speed limit in towns: 50kph/31mph.
- Seat belts must be worn in front seats at all times and in rear seats where fitted.
- There is a total ban on alcohol when driving. Random tests are quite common and police will issue on-the-spot fines.
- Fuel stations sell super and normal fuel (*benzin*), diesel (*mazot*) and unleaded fuel (*kursunşuz*). The price is extremely high. Credit cards are accepted. Service stations often have good toilets and are full service.
- If you break down driving your own car, call the Turkish Touring and Automobile Club (tel: Istanbul 0212 282 8140; fax 0212 282 8042; www. turing.org.tr). If your car is hired, follow the instructions you were given when hiring the vehicle. All accidents must be reported to the police. Don't move your car.

CAR RENTAL

Leading international car rental companies have offices in İzmir and all of the larger resorts. Many visitors book their car rental in advance from their home country. Drivers must be over 21 and have a valid driving licence.

Being there

TOURIST OFFICES

- Bodrum
  Bariş Meydanı 48
  ☎ 0252 316 1091

- Çanakkale
  Next to main dock
  ☎ 0217 0286 1187

- Fethiye
  İskele Karşısı 1
  ☎ 0252 614 1527

- İzmir
  Akdeniz Mah, 1344 Sok No 2,
  Pasaport
  ☎ 0232 483 6216/483 5117;
  www.izmir.turizm.gov.tr

- Kuşadası
  Liman Caddesi
  ☎ 0256 614 1103

- Marmaris
  İskele Meydanı 2
  ☎ 0252 412 1035

- Selçuk
  Atatürk Mah
  Efes Müzesi Karşısı
  ☎ 0232 892 1328;
  www.selcuk.gov.tr

There are also tourist offices in most towns of interest: see individual entries for addresses and telephone numbers.

MONEY

Turkey changed its currency in 2005, knocking off many noughts. The currency is the Yeni Turk Lira (YTL; new Turkish Lira). Coins *(kuruş)* are in 1, 5, 10, 20 *kuruş* and 1 YTL denominations. Notes are in 1, 5, 10, 20, 50 and 100YTL units. ATMs are everywhere and credit cards are widely accepted. Travellers' cheques have a discretionary commission if cashed at banks. Most tourist shops will quote in lira, euros, US dollars or pounds.

TIPS/GRATUITIES

Yes ✓ No ✗		
Restaurants (if service not included)	✓	10%
Cafés/bars (if service not included)	✓	change
Tour guides	✓	10–15%
Taxis	✓	round up fare
Chambermaids/hotel porters	✓	2–2.5YTL
Toilet attendants	✓	50 kuruş

POSTAL AND INTERNET SERVICES

Post offices (PTT) are easily recognizable by a black-on-yellow logo. In major resorts and larger towns the main PTT will stay open for phone calls until midnight. Open: 8am–7 or 8pm. Closed Sat pm and Sun. Stamps can only be purchased from post offices.

Internet cafés in major resorts open and close pretty quickly so look for a WiFi or Internet access sign at the popular bars in season. Smaller hotels may offer Internet access at a dedicated point in the building.

TELEPHONES

There are pay-phones on many streets, and at PTT offices. Phonecards are sold at post offices and newsagents. Most phones also accept credit cards. Main European mobile phones can be used here; North American visitors will need tri-band.

International dialling codes
UK: 00 44
Germany: 00 49
USA/Canada: 00 1
Netherlands: 00 31
Spain: 00 34

Emergency telephone numbers
Police: 155
Fire: 110
Ambulance: 112
Jandarma (military police): 156

EMBASSIES AND CONSULATES

UK ☎ 0232 463 5151
Germany ☎ 0232 488 8888
USA ☎ 0232 464 8755

Netherlands ☎ 0232 464 2201
Spain ☎ 0312 438 0392 (Ankara)

HEALTH ADVICE

Sun advice The sunniest and hottest months are July, August and September, with an average of 12 hours of sunshine and temperatures in the low 30s°C (80s/90s°F). During these months you should avoid the midday sun and use a strong sunblock and always drink plenty of water.
Drugs Prescription and non-prescription drugs and medicines are available from pharmacies *(eczane)*. They are able to dispense many drugs that would normally be available only on prescription in many countries.

Safe water Tap water is generally safe to drink, though it can be heavily chlorinated and taste unpleasant. Mineral water is inexpensive and is sold either sparkling *(maden suyu)* or still *(memba suyu)*.

PERSONAL SAFETY
The everyday police force in towns have blue uniforms. There are special tourist police in the major resorts who look the same but who should be able to speak some English and/or German. To help prevent crime:
● Do not carry more cash than you need
● Do not leave valuables on the beach or at the poolside
● Use safe boxes in your hotel
● Never leave anything of value in your car
Police assistance: tel: 155 from any call box

ELECTRICITY
The power supply in Turkey is 220 volts. Sockets take two-round-pin plugs but there are two sizes in use. Bring your own adaptor. Visitors from the USA will need a transformer. Power cuts are frequent in rural areas but usually short-lived.

OPENING HOURS

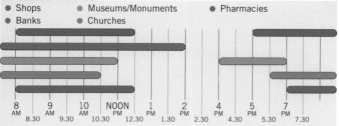

In addition to the times shown above, shops in tourist areas may open earlier and stay open for much longer, sometimes until midnight, every day of the week. Banks are closed on Saturdays and Sundays. Most have ATM machines with 24-hour access. Museums are usually closed on Mondays. Major post offices open Mon–Sat 8am–midnight, Sun 9–7. Minor post offices open Mon–Fri 8:30–12:30, 1:30–3:30. Many fuel stations open 24 hours, seven days a week.

LANGUAGE

Turkish is an extremely difficult language that builds sentences by adding suffixes to the basic word, and keeps the verb at the end. This can also alter the structure of the basic word and make it virtually unrecognizable to the untrained eye. Pronunciation *ai/ay* long i, eg side; *c* a hard j, eg jam; *ç* ch, eg chat; *ı* er/uh, eg letter; *ğ* y; *ü* ew, eg few (roughly); *ö* ur (more like the Scandinanvian ø); *j* zh (no English equivalent); *ş* sh, eg shut.

yes	*evet*	goodbye	*allahaısmarladık*
no	*hayır, yok*		*(said by the one*
please	*lütfen*		*leaving)*
thank you	*teşekkür ederim,*	goodbye	*güle güle (said by*
	mersi, sağol		*the one staying)*
you're welcome	*bir şey değil*	how much?	*ne kadar/kaça?*
excuse me	*özür dilerim*	open/closed	*açık/kapalı*
hello	*merhaba*	sorry	*pardon*
hotel/pension	*otel/pansiyon*	bath/shower	*banyo/duş*
single room	*tek kişilik oda*	toilet	*tuvalet*
double room	*iki kişilik oda*	hot water	*sıcak su*
one night	*bir gecelik*	key	*anahtar*
reservation	*reservasyon*	lift	*asansör*
room service	*oda servisi*	reception	*resepsiyon*
bank	*banka*	credit card	*kredi kart*
exchange office	*döriz*	exchange rate	*döviz kuru*
post office	*PTT or postane*	cashier	*kasiyer*
cheque	*çeki*	change	*bozuk para*
traveller's cheque	*seyahat çeki*	foreign currency	*doviz*
restaurant	*lokanta/restoran*	fruit	*meyva*
bill	*hesap*	bread	*ekmek*
breakfast	*kahvaltı*	beer/wine	*bira/şarap*
appetisers	*meze*	ice	*buz*
dessert	*tatlı*	water	*su*
yoghurt drink	*ayran*	mineral water	*maden suyu*
tea/coffee	*çay/kahve*	milk	*süt*

Best places to see

1 Afrodisias Stadium

Stadia adorn many of Turkey's ancient sites, but none can compare with the one at Afrodisias, which is the best-preserved example of its kind.

The word 'stadium' comes from a measurement of about 200m (656ft), the distance of the shortest foot race in ancient Greece and which over time came to be used for the public arena where races and other games took place. The stadium of Afrodisias stretches for just over 263m (863ft) and its 25 rows of seats could accommodate 30,000 spectators. Its excellent state of preservation owes a great deal to the Turkish professor Kenan Erim and his team at New York University, who effectively resurrected Afrodisias between 1961 and his death in 1990. The stadium had been buried as a result of earthquakes in the Middle Ages and from the 13th century onwards the whole of Afrodisias had been abandoned and more or less forgotten about by the world.

It is best to follow the path that leads round the site, going first to the theatre and then to the Odeon and Temple of Aphrodite on the right. A little way past this the path heads north for 200m (220yds) to reach the spectacular stadium. The Romans were keen to emulate the Greek tradition

of holding sporting and artistic competitions to mark religious festivals and the impressive scale of this stadium shows how much importance was attached to public entertainment.

The stadium was the scene of a major festival and sporting competitions, and as well as the traditional Greek events – foot races, wrestling, boxing and the pentathlon – the Romans also staged chariot races and gladiatorial combats.

➕ P14 ✉ 40km (25 miles) southeast of Nazilli, off the main Aydın–Denizli road ⏰ Summer daily 8:30–7; winter daily 8:30–5 💷 Moderate 🍴 Anatolia Restaurant, Geyre Kasabası (££) on the road to Karacasu, 13km (8 miles) to the west 🚌 *Dolmuş*/minibus from Karacasu or Nazilli ❓ Tours from Kuşadası and other resorts

2 # Bodrum Kalesi (Castle of St Peter)

www.bodrum-museum.com

This grand example of 15th-century crusader architecture dominates Bodrum harbour and houses the Museum of Underwater Archaeology.

The Knights Hospitallers of St John, militant anti-Muslim Christians, arrived in Bodrum in 1402 and set about choosing a site for a mighty fortress. The first of its double curtain walls was completed in 1437, but building work continued until 1522; shortly thereafter the Knights were forced to evacuate because Süleyman the Magnificent captured their headquarters in Rhodes. Inside the main castle there were separate towers for the English, French, Italian and German contingents,

each proudly displaying its own coat of arms.

The Museum of Underwater Archaeology contains an invaluable collection of some of the world's oldest ships, such as the 14th-century BC Uluburun Wreck. The Glass Wreck Hall (separate admission charge) contains a carefully preserved seventh-century Byzantine trading ship alongside its cargo of glass. The *Carian Princess* (separate admission charge) is named after the royal occupant of a sarcophagus that was discovered in 1989, and dates from *c*360BC. It is suggested that the princess was the wife or sister of King Mausolus.

The English Tower has been restored in a mock-medieval style. Armour and trophies decorate the walls, and staff in medieval costumes sell glasses of wine.

Climb to the top of the castle, above the *Carian Princess* room, for wide views of Bodrum and the harbour. A morbid area includes the dungeons, restored and embellished with ghoulish scenes and sound effects.

➕ K16 ✉ Bodrum, behind the tourist information office
☎ 0252 316 2516 🕓 Tue–Sun 8:30–12, 2–5 (longer hours in Jul and Aug). Shorter hours for some exhibits
✋ Moderate to expensive, depending how many sections are visited 🍴 Café (£) inside the castle; many on the quay outside

3 Çeşme

A low-key, relaxing resort on the coast, with Ottoman architecture and thermal springs, Çeşme has managed to avoid the worst excesses of tourism.

Many of the houses close to Çeşme's seafront are well-preserved 19th-century homes, and an evening wander through the streets is very rewarding. The word *çeşme* (pronounced *cheshma*) means 'fountain', and a number of old Ottoman fountains still exist in the town. People come to Çeşme for its water: there are therapeutic thermal springs in the area and you can benefit from these at some of the local hotels. Delightful decorated balconies adorn many of the Ottoman buildings, and there are two 18th-century mosques. A 16th-century Ottoman fortress dominates the town and is now home to a small, rather uninspiring museum.

Çeşme is not as blatantly touristy as resorts like Bodrum and Kuşadası, but the town has still developed a modest entertainment infrastructure for visitors. Any of the agencies dotted around town can arrange a day trip to Chios, and a longer trip to Italy via Brindisi is also possible. There is a

Turkish bath in the centre of town, and although
Çeşme itself is quiet at night, the surrounding area
has a number of lively discos and pubs.

Ilica, 4km (2.5 miles) to the east, is the liveliest
place for evening entertainment, and has several
spas and the best beach in the vicinity. The beach
at Boyalık is more exposed, but hot springs in the
seabed help compensate for any chill in the air.

➕ B8 ✉ 80km (50 miles) west of İzmir 🕔 Castle and
museum: summer Tue–Sun 8:30–7:30; winter Tue–Sun
8:30–11:45, 1–5:15 ✋ Castle and museum inexpensive
🍴 Restaurants (£–££) along the seafront 🚌 *Dolmuş/*
minibus from İzmir 🚢 Greek island of Chios, 9km (5.5 miles)
offshore
ℹ️ Near the pier ☎ 0232 712 6653 🕔 Jul–Sep Mon–Fri
8:30–7; Oct–Apr daily 8:30–12, 1–5

4 Efes (Ephesus) Theatre

This great Roman theatre had seating for 24,000. From the top row there is an unsurpassed view of ancient Ephesus.

In the AD60s a real life drama was played out here when St Paul's preaching sparked off an anti-Christian demonstration (Acts 19:24–41). A pagan silversmith named Demetrius accused the Christians of disrespect for the goddess Artemis and a riot broke out. Paul left shortly afterwards, leaving Demetrius and others to recover their trade in Artemis merchandise. Their successors may be seen peddling Artemis schlock in the many stalls that line the entrance to Ephesus.

In classical Greece, theatres had no stage: all the action took place in the orchestra. In Hellenistic times a small stage was introduced, and the Romans doubled this in size to some 6m (20ft) in depth. Hence the decorated double row of columns and single row of pilasters, which are still standing – they once supported the stage.

From the stage area, with its various entrances, it is clear how the auditorium gradually gets steeper, designed as it was to provide good views for those in the inexpensive seats at the back. In the auditorium itself, listen to people talking in the stage area: the acoustics are still excellent, though the Greeks and Romans also placed bronze and clay sounding boards at strategic spots. From the higher rows there is a superb view of the road now known as the Arcadian Way. The reedy grass at its far end indicates what was once the line of the harbour.

✚ *Ephesus b2* ✉ 3km (2 miles) from Selçuk ☎ 0232 892 6402/6940 🕐 Daily 8–6:30 (5:30 in winter) ✋ Moderate 🍴 Restaurants (not recommended) at the Lower Entrance. Bring a picnic or eat in Selçuk (➤ 125) 🚌 Buses to Selçuk from Kuşadası and İzmir. Taxis and free shuttles drive up to the top for an easier walk down through the site ❓ Tours from most resorts ℹ️ Atatürk Mah, Selçuk ☎ 0232 892 6328 🕐 Mon–Fri 8:30–5:30, Sat–Sun 9–5 in summer

5 Hierapolis

Roman architecture on a grand scale dominates Hierapolis. The theatre is vast, and the necropolis was one of the biggest in Asia Minor.

The King of Pergamum (➤ 50–51), Eumenes II, developed Hierapolis in the second century BC, but the monuments that attract visitors today were constructed by the Romans after they inherited the town. The name means Holy City, and the town was associated from the start with the mysterious Springs of Pamukkale (➤ 48–49), part of the same site. To appreciate the scale of the Roman theatre, take a seat in the very top row. Go down into the theatre orchestra, which gives access to the fine reliefs behind the stage. The lower ones can be admired at close quarters.

After leaving the theatre, if time permits, turn to the right and continue up the unpaved track to pass remains of the city walls, before turning left for the ruins of the Martyrion of St Philip. If time is limited, head back to the car park from the theatre and turn right to reach the colonnaded Frontinus Street. This splendidly preserved Roman street begins just after the Motel Koru on the other side of the road. Frontinus Street is 4m (13ft) wide and at the north end has a monumental gate, dedicated to the emperor Domitian in AD84. As you walk towards the Domitian Arch look for the well-preserved Roman public toilets on the right. Continue through the Domitian Arch to the large necropolis, dotted with lavish tombs. The Roman baths contain a museum.

✚ P13 ✉ Pamukkale, 19km (12miles) north of Denizli 🎟 Museum: Tue–Sun 8–12, 12:30–6. Site ticket office: 8–7. Rest of site open 24 hours, but no light at night 👊 Moderate 🍴 Café by Antique Pool for drinks and snacks (£) 🚌 Dolmuş/minibus from Denizli every 20 mins, long-distance bus from Marmaris, Kuşadası, Fethiye and other towns
ℹ Opposite the museum ☎ 0258 272 2077 🕐 Daily 8–12, 1:30–5:30 (1:30–5 in winter)

6 Ölüdeniz

The soft, sandy beach, with a backdrop of pine-forests, is over 3km (2 miles) long, and the water in the lagoon is transparent – avoid high season.

The name of Turkey's most beautiful beach setting means 'dead sea', referring to the calmness of the water, which is almost completely cut off. Ölüdeniz is a warm, sheltered lagoon that manages to be magnificent, despite the lack of a view of the open sea and over-development of the surrounding hills. At the height of summer it is packed with people; out of season, there is little that can compare. The setting is superb: the beaches stretch for such a distance that it is usually possible to find some space. The prettiest stretch of beach winds around the lagoon, but it is closed off and requires a separate entrance fee. This beach proves popular with Turkish families, while other holidaymakers seem to prefer the long stretch of Belceğiz.

Despite the popularity of Ölüdeniz, some efforts have been made to preserve the pristine beauty of its waters. Yachts are forbidden to use its sheltered location, and an attempt has been made to contain the most rampant development of giant resorts; most local hotels are relatively low key. Nevertheless, hotel advertising boards spoil the approach to Ölüdeniz from Fethiye.

The protected water of the lagoon is ideal for safe canoeing and kayaks are readily available for hire. At night, there is plenty of opportunity for partying at nightspots in nearby Ovacık and Hisarönü, but the food scene is dismal, despite the proliferation of restaurants. Take a picnic lunch if you are going for the day.

✚ P17 ✉ 15km (9 miles) south of Fethiye ✋ Paying beach (inexpensive) 🍴 Restaurants (£–££) fronting the beach
🚌 *Dolmuş*/minibus from Fethiye

Pamukkale

The spring pool that attracted the Romans is now part of a motel. Swim here among the submerged columns of an ancient portico.

Hot spring water cools as it comes to the surface on the edge of a plateau, some 100m (330ft) above the Lycos Valley, and as the dissolved calcium bicarbonate gives off carbon dioxide, the remaining calcium carbonate solidifies. The prosaic chemistry does scant justice to the place: what it means is that the water runs down a series of bright white terraces of precipitated chalk formed into irregular pools, odd shapes and stalactites.

From the valley below, you see the high plateau swathed on one side with white cliffs. Hence the name Pamukkale, or 'cotton castle'. On the plateau above the ancient town of Hierapolis, Pamukkale developed because of the springs, which were considered holy, and the Romans established a health spa. So many visitors have followed in their footsteps that measures have belatedly been taken to protect the natural formation. Tourists are only permitted to paddle in one small area, without shoes, but there are still obvious signs of deterioration in the pools.

Stay a night to take in the strange beauty of the place as evening falls. The Antique Pool is truly remarkable, containing a collection of fallen masonry from

ancient Hierapolis (➤ 44–45). Get here early to enjoy a swim before the afternoon tour buses arrive and disgorge a flood of visitors.

🕂 P13 ✉ 19km (12 miles) north of Denizli ☎ 0258 261 3393 ✋ Moderate 🍴 Café serving drinks and snacks by the Antique Pool (£); otherwise picnic or eat in Karahayit village 🚌 *Dolmuş*/minibus from Denizli every 20 mins, long-distance bus from Marmaris, Kuşadası, Fethiye and other towns ❓ Tours combining Pamukkale and Hierapolis from most major resorts
🛈 Opposite the museum ☎ 0258 268 6539/ 272 2077
🕐 Daily 8–12, 1:30–7:30 (1:30–5:30 in winter)

8 Pergamum

The two great attractions here are the acropolis, a majestic statement of political might, and the Asklepeion, devoted to the art of healing.

Pergamum emerged as a powerful force in Hellenistic times, but the last king, Attalus III, was so keen to placate the Romans that he bequeathed the kingdom to Rome in 133BC. It remained an important city and today there is plenty to see. An organized tour that includes transport and a guide is a good bet because the acropolis is 8km (5 miles) from the Asklepeion, and both sites contain several points of interest. Otherwise, take a taxi from one

site to the other and invest in a specialist guidebook.

On the acropolis, the Greek theatre is unusually steep, with 80 rows of seats carved into the hillside. Post holes to the rear of the orchestra still show where temporary scenery was erected as a backdrop to the drama. The partly restored Temple of Trajan evokes the grandeur of the site under the Romans, but its art treasures, the relief carvings on the Temple of Zeus, were moved to the Pergamon Museum in Berlin in the 19th century.

At the far end of the modern town of Bergama, the Asklepeion was the leading medical centre of the ancient world. Patients slept in the sanctuary, hoping to be cured by divine influence, and had their dreams interpreted by priestly physicians who prescribed baths in the sacred water that still flows here. The remains of a circular Temple of Zeus are worth seeing, and there is a small, well-preserved theatre in the northwest corner. In the southwest corner are remains of the public latrines.

✚ D6 ✉ Acropolis: 6km (4 miles) north of Bergama. Asklepeion: 2km (1.2 miles) south of Bergama 🕓 Acropolis and Asklepeion; daily 8:30–7 (closes 5:30 in winter) ✋ Moderate 🍴 Restaurants (£) in Bergama 🚌 Buses to Bergama from Ayvalık and İzmir
ℹ Bergama Tourist Office ☎ 0232 631 2851 🕓 Summer daily 8:30–7; winter Mon–Fri 8:30–12, 12:30–5:30

Rock Tombs, Fethiye

The ancient Lycian people left tantalizing traces. When an earthquake flattened Fethiye in 1957, the Lycian rock tombs remained intact.

Fethiye stands on the site of the Lycian port of Telmessos. All that remains of the ancient town is its tombs, cut into the rock overlooking Fethiye. Try to visit near sunset when the climb up is less exhausting and when there is the bonus of panoramic views. Steep steps lead up to the most impressive site, the Tomb of Amyntas, a temple-like structure with twin Ionic columns between two pilasters adorned with rosettes at the top. A fading inscription on the left pilaster records that the tomb belonged to Amyntas, and gives the name of his father. Nothing else is known about the family or the fourth century BC building. The main chamber has a door with four panels, which still have their original iron studs, although tomb robbers have broken in at some time in the past. The iron studs are imitations of the bronze nails which adorned the wooden porches of Greek temples.

➕ *Fethiye d3* ✉ Fethiye 🕐 Daily 8:30–sunset
✋ Moderate 🍴 Restaurants in town (£–££) and a café (£) opposite the entrance 🚌 Buses to Fethiye from Bodrum, Denizli, İzmir, Marmaris, Ölüdeniz, Pamukkale and Patara
ℹ Near harbour, İskele Karşısı ☎ 0252 614 1527

10 Xanthos, Harpy Tomb

British 'archaeologists' took two months in 1842 to pillage Xanthos of its art treasures, but the site is still capable of stirring the imagination.

Start your visit to this ancient city by taking a seat in the Roman theatre, and gazing down on the orchestra, which is still full of fallen masonry from the stage and its columned facade. The experience evokes an impressive feeling for the history of the site.

To the west of the theatre stand two Lycian pillar tombs, the Harpy Tomb (545BC) and, alongside it, a twin sarcophagus. The bas-relief at the top of the 5m-high (16ft) pillared Harpy Tomb carries plaster copies of the marble originals, now in the British Museum in London. They show seated figures receiving gifts, with bird-like, winged women carrying children in their arms on the north and south sides. These images were once thought to

represent the mythical creatures known as Harpies, hideous winged monsters, personifying hurricanes and tornadoes (in Greek the word means 'snatcher'). Modern theories tend to suggest, however, that they are actually carvings of the Sirens, part women, part birds, who lured seafarers to their deaths with their enchanted singing. Here they are carrying away dead souls in the form of children. The adjacent, twin sarcophagus dates from the third century BC. It is not known why the tombs were put on top of each other in this unusual manner.

✚ Q18 ✉ Just north of Kınık, 63km (40 miles) from Fethiye
🕓 May–Oct daily 8:30–7; Nov–Apr daily 8:30–5:30
✋ Moderate 🍴 Café (£) across the road, but it's best to bring a picnic 🚌 *Dolmuş*/minibus from Fethiye or Kalkan

Best things to do

Great places to have lunch

Agora (£)
The smartest of the small number of restaurants in Herakleia, serving Turkish and some Western dishes in a pleasant outdoor setting under shade.
✉ Herakleia ☎ 0252 543 5445

La Dolce Vita (££)
Air-conditioned comfort in which to sample pizza and Caesar salad from an international menu. Some tables are placed near the street for outdoor dining.
✉ Hilton Hotel, Gaziosmanpasa Bulvarı, İzmir ☎ 0232 441 6060

Gusta (££)
There's a lovely shaded waterfront terrace at this contemporary Mediterranean restaurant which offers seafood, pizzas and salads. The dining room is bright and chic, but long lunches are so much better in the open air.
✉ Waterfront Gümüşlük, Bodrum Peninsula ☎ 0252 394 4228

Kalehan (£)
The only restaurant in Selçuk with some character to its surroundings, plus the comfort of air-conditioning and good Turkish food. The à la carte menu changes daily, the four-course set meals are good value, and there is a wine list.
✉ Kalehan Hotel, Atatürk Caddesi 49, Selçuk
☎ 0232 892 6154

Körfez (£)
This sea-facing restaurant has a large menu but it is the fish or fish-based dishes which are the most tempting. There is an impressive selection of *meze*, as well as

the main fish dishes. There are also 'International cuisine
selections' for those who prefer chicken curry or steak and chips.
✉ Seafront, Çeşme ☎ 0232 712 6718

Labranda

Take a picnic with you up to the remote ruins at Labranda
(▶ 164). The road is not easy but the rewards are truly
spectacular with cool shaded woodland fringing vast panoramas.
✉ 21km (13 miles) off the Milas–Selçuk road

Ocakbaş (£)

Dine on the terrace in one of the most beautiful inland villages of
the Aegean coast. The menu here offers traditional dishes,
including delicious light *gözleme* pancakes.
✉ İki Kilisi Arasında, Şirince, Selçuk ☎ 0232 898 3094

Rihtim (£)

There are other restaurants alongside the Rihtim, but this is one of
the longer-established places on the quayside street facing the
Dardanelles. The speciality is fish, served with salad and chips.
✉ Çanakkale ☎ 0286 217 1770

Riverside (££)

Overlooking the languid waters of the Dalyan River
across from the cliffside tombs of Kaunos, Riverside
offers inspiring views from its verdant terrace and tasty
cuisine from its professional chef/owner Sami.
✉ Riverfront, Dalyan ☎ 0252 284 3107

Sardis (Sart) (£)

Have lunch with the Turkish truck drivers at one of the
köfte restaurants near Salihli. You eat what you are
given – sausage, *köftesı* (meatballs) and bread.
✉ Near Salihli, 9km (5.5 miles) from Sardis

Top activities

Boating: hire a boat, join a cruise or charter a boat with a crew.

Go underwater: use a snorkel or dive – resorts have facilities for all levels of experience.

Swim: huge choice of beaches (➤ 72–73).

Visit ancient sites: Ephesus (➤ 42–43) and other popular sites have the most to see, but less famous ones may have more atmosphere.

Visit a Greek island: for example Rhodes from Marmaris (➤ 166–169).

Shop: all day and half the night. Shops stay open late (➤ 32).

Watch the wildlife: loggerhead turtles on beaches, storks on buildings, lizards and tortoises at ancient sites, wild flowers everywhere.

Horse-riding
Horse Safari & Horse Camp
A way for older children and adults to see the landscape from a different point of view. Bodrum's Country Ranch offers individual riding lessons, 1- to 2-hour trips and trekking.
Country Ranch
✉ Turgutreis ☎ 0252 382 5654

Walking
Although most of the serious walking in Turkey is done in the central mountains, this can still be a rewarding activity in the coastal regions, providing a glimpse of older, more traditional ways of life, away from the busy resorts. Unfortunately, mapping is poor, so navigation can be difficult. Be wary of the heat and the

sun, especially during the middle of the day. Wear a hat and take plenty of water.

Saklıkent

This 18km-long (11-mile) gorge, so narrow in places that the sun doesn't reach it, makes an appealing day out for more experienced walkers. A wooden boardwalk takes you some of the way, but the walk also involves a little wading and scrambling. Bring a picnic, although there are places to eat should you want them.

✉ Saklıkent, 46km (29 miles) southeast of Fethiye 🕐 Daily 8–5
🚌 *Dolmuş*/minibus to Fethiye

Long-distance trail

The Lycian Way is a 509km (316-mile) walking trail from Fethiye through the mountains to Antalya. It is clearly marked and there is an accompanying guidebook and excellent website that offer suggestions on where to stay and eat. It is possible to do a small section: the end near Fethiye is easiest; www.lycianway.com.

Watersports and adventure tours

Windsurfing, parasailing, jet-skiing and canoeing are the most popular activities, and snorkelling, under supervision, is enthralling for children. Check what your travel insurance says about accidents involving watersports. In the bigger resorts it is worth asking whether the agencies that handle boat trips can also arrange activities such as trekking, canoeing or rafting. Older children are usually accepted, if they have an adult with them.

Borda ✉ Neyzen Tevfir Caddesi 48, Bodrum ☎ 0252 313 7767; www.bordayachting.com

Best Turkish baths and massage

The traditional *hamam* has separate days for male and female customers, using male and female masseurs respectively.

NORTHERN AEGEAN
Çeşme
Sheraton Çeşme Hotel Resort and Spa
The largest spa along the coast with thermal treatments alongside current mainstream and traditional therapies.

✉ Sifne Caddesi 35, Ilica ☎ 0232 723 1240 🕓 Daily 8am–10pm

Kuşadası
Belediye
Situated across from the old mosque and featuring traditional mixed bathing.

✉ Yildirmit Caddesi ☎ 0256 614 1219 🕓 Daily 9–9

Kaleiçi Hamanı
If you fail to make a visit, warns the cute advertisement, 'we will think that you don't like your body'. Located behind the post office.

✉ Camikebir Mah Eyul Sokak 17 ☎ 0256 614 1292 🕓 Daily 9–9

Pamukkale
Spa Hotel Colossae Thermal
Offers a day spa and short-term residential (up to 7 days) regime advice at a state-of-the-art spa and thermal therapy complex.

✉ Karahayıt Mevkii ☎ 0258 271 4156 🕓 Daily 8am–9pm

Selçuk
Hamam
The *hamam* is in the centre of town, next door to the police station. Mixed bathing and a soft massage.

✉ Sokak 2002 ☎ 0232 892 6198 🕓 Mid-morning to 10pm

SOUTHERN AEGEAN
Bodrum
Hamam

This is a more traditional *hamam* than you might expect for Bodrum. Wednesday and Saturday afternoons are set aside for women only.

✉ Dere Umucra Sokak ⏰ Daily 8–5

Fethiye
Hamam

Although the *hamam* itself dates back to the 16th century, this is a touristy establishment and one that most Turkish people would turn their noses up at.

✉ Hamam Sokak 20 ☎ 0252 614 9318; www.oldturkishbath. com ⏰ Daily 7am–midnight

Marmaris
Sultan Hamam

Aimed at the tourist market, with women-only and men-only baths, as well as a mixed one and a choice of massages.

✉ Taşlik Centre ☎ 0252 413 6850 ⏰ Daily 8am–midnight

a walk around Efes (Ephesus)

From the ticket office walk straight ahead to the marble-paved path.

The theatre is on the left, and on the right is the Arcadian Way, one of the few streets outside Rome to have streetlighting in ancient times.

Go to the theatre (➤ 42–43) and climb the steps. You can go straight to the theatre's seating area, or turn right near the top of the steps and enter the theatre orchestra through the roofed passageway to find the seats rising up the hillside in front of you. Leave the theatre on the opposite side.

About halfway along the marble-paved street, look for the brothel sign (a footprint and a female face) etched on a pavement stone on the right side, protected by a metal frame.

At the end of this street, the two-storey facade of the Library of Celsus (➤ 90–91) is on the right. Turn left, up a gradually sloping marble-paved street.

Look for the Roman public toilets on the left and the ancient spice shop. Next comes Hadrian's Temple. Inside the temple entrance, on the right side, note the 13 carved figures on the walls: Athena and other deities alongside a Roman family. The originals and an explanation are in the Ephesus Museum in Selçuk (➤ 114).

Carry on up the street until a sign points right to the museum of inscriptions.

The delightful odeon (theatre) up on the left makes an ideal picnic stop. You can leave from the Upper Entrance, just ahead, or retrace your route to the Lower Entrance.

Distance 2km/1 mile (4km/2.5 miles if returning to start point)
Time 3–4 hours
Start point Lower Entrance ✚ *Ephesus b1*
End point Upper Entrance/Lower Entrance
✚ *Ephesus d3/Ephesus b1*
Lunch The restaurants at the Lower Entrance are not recommended. Bring a picnic and, on a hot day, plenty of water. Restaurants in Selçuk (➤ 125)

Places to take the children

Turkey doesn't have many attractions specifically designed for children, but it is a welcoming place for them all the same.

Most of the better resort hotels will have a children's pool separate from the main pool. Some hotels, usually in co-operation with a tour operator in your own country, have special clubs for children (3- to 6-year-olds and 7- to 12-year-olds) – effectively taking them off your hands for morning and afternoon sessions. Babysitting in the evening is not very easy to arrange.

CAMEL RIDES
Rides on a small group of camels along the beach at Kagı on the Bodrum peninsula during the summer.

MUD BATHS
Kids can revel in the mud at Köyceğiz. They won't care if it has therapeutic qualities – it's just great fun.

THE OPEN SEA
Getting there is half the fun, and a journey across open sea to a Greek island is enjoyable for all ages. Ferries operate between:
Çeşme and Chios; Ayvalık and Lesbos; Kuşadası and Sámos; Bodrum and Kos; and Bodrum/Marmaris and Rhodes.

PARKS
Kültürpark, İzmir
This is the main park in İzmir and is home to a zoo and amusement park as well as a restaurant and quiet gardens. It is also the site of the İzmir International Fair, but for most of the year it's a welcome oasis in the centre of the city.

WATERPARKS
Aquafantasy, Kuşadası
A 5-star beach hotel with an elaborate aquapark, also open to day visitors.

✉ Ephesus Beach, Pamucak, between Kuşadası and Selçuk ☎ 0233 893 1111; www.aquafantasy.com
🕐 Apr–Oct daily

Aquapark Dedeman
There are waterslides and pools at this fun waterpark next to the Dedeman Hotel, 3km (2 miles) from Bodrum town centre.
For adults there are bars and restaurants in the hotel.

✉ Dedeman Hotel, Turgutreis Yölü
☎ 0252 358 6161 🕐 Daily 9am–10pm

Atlantis Aquapark and Aquapark İçmeler
The Atlantis Aquapark is a water-based fun park for children with waterslides, a 'froggy island' and there's a bar for parents. Aquapark İçmeler, under the same management as Atlantis, is on the right as you enter İçmeler from Marmaris.

✉ Sitler Mah, 212 Sok 3 Uzunyalı, Marmaris ☎ 0252 411 6162
🕐 Morning to evening

Best buys and best bazaars

BEST BUYS

Carpets are sold everywhere. Turkish carpets have an international reputation, but there are many differences in quality. Whether a carpet is handwoven or machine-made is fundamental to its value; other things that matter are the density of the knots in handwoven carpets, whether the dyes are either natural or cheaper chemical ones, and whether the carpet is made of wools or silk. The flat-woven, double-sided mats known as *kilims* are always less expensive.

Ceramic plates, bowls, jugs and pots come in vivid blues and greens with abstract designs.

A **brass tea tray,** complete with tiny tea glasses.

Food and drink: pine-scented honey, bags of pine nuts, gift-wrapped pastries, Turkish delight, a bottle or two of *raki.*

Leather jackets, coats, shoes, bags and belts.

Meerschaum is a soft white magnesium silicate from western Anatolia, carved by craftsmen into pipes and figurines.

Onyx is best purchased from a workshop where you can see it being cut and shaped. Inexpensive, but very heavy.

An **Ottoman-style** souvenir, perhaps a water pipe, copperware or jewellery.

BEST BAZAARS
Kuşadası, Bodrum and Marmaris

Kuşadası, Bodrum and Marmaris all have bazaars *(basar* in Turkish). Resort bazaars consist of small shops on either side of a pedestrianized street or passageway, many with awnings. The advantage is a high density of tourist-orientated shops, all competing with one another, and the cool shade of the awnings can be welcome in the high season. The drawback is that the constant importuning by proprietors, and roaming touts can be tiresome. The sales line usually begins with an offer of tea, but such hospitality comes naturally to Turkish people and no commitment is being sought when the offer is made.

The merchandise covers a wide range, especially in Marmaris. Shops selling leather clothing and goods – handbags, travel bags, briefcases, accessories – are all over the place, followed closely by stores selling carpets and *kilims*, jewellery, meerschaum pipes, ceramics and crafts.

Check out some of the clothes stores with familiar branded North American and European labels, as these are usually made under licence in Turkey and are often much less expensive than back home. The least expensive items in a bazaar will usually be souvenirs, synthetic apple tea powder, sandals and beachwear, Turkish delight *(lokum)* and other types of confectionery.

İzmir

The maze of narrow streets and cul-de-sacs to the north of Konak Square make up the city's bazaar. It's easy to get lost, so try and check where you are going (see guided walk, ➤ 100–101).

The countless shops, stalls and workshops are used by Turks rather than tourists, and the clothes and shoe shops are well worth looking into, as are the music shops where the traditional folk music scene flourishes. The atmosphere is the main attraction: it is a place of great interest and character and still the best place to immerse yourself in the sounds, sights and smells of Turkish culture. Don't go on a Sunday, when most of the shops are closed.

Stunning views

Looking down across the Aegean Sea to the Greek island of Lesbos (Lésvos) from the ancient site of the citadel of Assos.

From the viewpoint at the upper edge of the field of dazzling limestone pools that make up the Cotton Castle at Pamukkale.

Standing at the top of Curetes Street looking down on the ancient city of Ephesus. Your eye is drawn to the magnificent facade of the Library of Celsus at the bottom of the hill.

The ancient Lycian rock tombs of Kaunos cut high in the cliffside above the Dalyan River, beautifully accented by the verdant foliage of the riverbanks below.

Up along the meandering empty cobbled streets of Kayaköy, a ghost town abandoned by its Greek population during the exchange of populations between Greeks and Turks after World War I.

The narrow whitewashed streets of Bodrum's old town. The walls of its old mansions and fishermen's houses are festooned with souvenirs and it's thronging with people into the early hours of the morning.

The view across the masts of yachts moored in Bodrum marina to the crenellated walls of St Peter's Castle on the hillside, especially at night when the castle is floodlit.

The golden teardrop beach contrasting with ebony dark waters of Ölüdeniz.

Views across the terracotta-tiled rooftops to the *gülets* along the harbourfront from the walls of the hilltop castle at Marmaris.

The exquisite multi-columned entrance vestibule to the temple of the oracle at Didim.

Best beaches

Western Turkey has plenty of beaches for young children who are happy to build sandcastles and play under supervision in shallow water. It can sometimes be difficult to find shady places on the sand, though, so remember hats, sunblock and other protection from the sun.

Always check with your hotel and the local tourist office about the advisability of swimming off the local beach: don't assume it will be safe. Apart from undertows and difficult currents, some stretches of sea are sometimes just too polluted to be healthy. The beaches at Calış (➤ 150) and Turgutreis (➤ 139) are safe in so far as the sea there is shallow for a long way out. This is also true of the beach at İztuzu (Dalyan ➤ 150–151), which is a nesting site for loggerhead turtles.

Alaçatı Beach – Çeşme: The strong prevailing breezes offshore here make it a favourite with windsurfers and kitesurfers, so it attracts the cool sporting crowds.

Altinkum: The town beach sits directly at the head of the town main street so it's perfect for combining sunbathing with lunch and a little shopping.

Calış Beach – Fethiye: A long ribbon of sand backed by hotels, cafés and lokantas with great water sports to enjoy.

İztuzu: A long fine stretch set at the mouth of the Dalyan River and one of the last turtle nesting sites in the Eastern Mediterranean.

Kagı – Bodrum: Golden sand, palms and even camel rides on this bay on the Bodrum peninsula.

Ladies Beach (Kadinlar Plaji) – Kuşadası: One of the busiest along the coast but a great place for the singles social scene.

Long Beach – Kuşadası: It's a 6km (4-mile) strip of sand with excellent water sports, bungee rides and lots of cafés for a cold beer or coke.

Ölüdeniz: Set in the lee of sheer pine-clad cliffs, is Turkey's most famous stretch of sand. A perfect teardrop of sand gently shelving into a deep limpid sheltered pool.

Marmaris: The town beach stretches off, seemingly forever, north along the edge of the bay. It's now lined with a never-ending string of hotels, but what a location.

Patara: Turkey's longest single beach at 18km (11 miles) and one of the least developed on the west coast. The vast dunes that back the beach swamp the remains of a Roman city and turtles nest on the foreshore.

Exploring

Western Turkey invites exploration. There are countless ancient archaeological sites, numerous golden beaches, vast agricultural valleys, pine-clad hills, and bustling towns where you can visit the museums or enjoy a spot of shopping – it's almost a national sport here. Several highlights stand out, but you'll find something interesting around every corner, be it a stunning Roman amphitheatre, cotton fields like a carpet of snow, or a Lycian tomb standing sentinel against fragrant wild herb scrub.

A well-organized tourist infrastructure means you don't have to work hard to get around. Local buses are cheap and efficient, and if you can't get there by land, you can be sure that there are plenty of boat trips from the local harbour. Book an organized tour or do your own thing. It's certain that you won't regret leaving the poolside.

Northern Aegean

There is so much to see. The chief resort is Kuşadası, one of the liveliest anywhere along the Turkish coast and well placed for day trips to major sites such as Ephesus, Pamukkale and Hierapolis. The city of İzmir (ancient Smyrna) is attractive, though somewhat hectic. It is a good place in which to experience the urban Turkish culture that resort towns lack. İzmir is also a convenient base for a visit to the idyllic Temple of Artemis, near the site of ancient Sardis, home to the fabulously rich King Croesus in the sixth century BC.

İzmir

To the north of İzmir is ancient Pergamum, easiest to visit on an organized tour. Further north again lies the town of Çanakkale,

which overlooks the Dardanelles, very prominent in history and mythology. The World War I battlefields of Gallipoli are just across the water, and Homer's Troy is just a short day trip away inland.

AFRODİSİAS

This ancient site was associated with fertility cults from as early as the Bronze Age, and the Greeks named it Aphrodisias after their goddess of love, Aphrodite. A temple dedicated to her stood here in the eighth century BC. The Romans transformed Aphrodisias into a major cultural centre, and held sculpture competitions: sculptors were especially attracted to the place because of the quality of the local marble.

Parts of the site are periodically closed off for restoration work, but enough is always left open to make a visit rewarding. There is a stadium (► 36–37), a well-preserved Roman theatre, the Baths of Hadrian complete with floor tiles, and the Temple of Aphrodite, which survived its conversion into a basilica during the Byzantine era. Leave time to visit the museum with its extensive collection of sculptures.

✚ P14 ✉ 40km (25 miles) southeast of Nazilli, off the main Aydın–Denizli road ⊙ Summer daily 8:30–7; winter daily 8:30–5 ✋ Moderate ▓ Restaurants (£–££) in Karacasu, 13km (8 miles) to the west ☐ *Dolmuş*/minibus from Karacasu or Nazilli ? Tours from Kuşadası and other resorts

AFRODİSİAS STADIUM

Best places to see, ► 36–37.

ALİNDA

This little-visited ancient site has impressive ruins, and the setting, on the steep eastern slopes of Mount Latmus, is delightful. Alexander the Great came here and helped the Queen of Halicarnassos (Bodrum, ► 129), then in exile, regain her throne in 334BC. The chief ruin is a huge and remarkably well-preserved market building. Higher up, the small theatre is overgrown but has also survived well. It is worth seeking out for an unrivalled view over the village of Karpuzla and the pretty valley formed by the River Çine Çayı. Higher still is a watchtower, surrounded by tunnels, partly open, that lead down the hillside.

✚ L14 ✉ 25km (15.5 miles) to the west of the Aydın–Muğla main road 🖐 Inexpensive 🍴 Restaurants (£) in Karpuzla 🚌 *Dolmuş*/minibus from Aydın

ASSOS

The ruins of the city of Assos stand on a cliff above the pretty fishing port of Behramkale. Founded by Greek colonists in the eighth century BC, Assos was so renowned as an intellectual centre that the philosopher Aristotle lived here for three years. The town was later captured by his pupil, Alexander the Great. The highlight is the partly reconstructed Temple of Athena (530BC) with its spectacular view of Lesbos, the starting point of the original Greek colonists. There are also well-preserved sections of the fourth century BC city walls, over 12m (39ft) high in places, and a necropolis with an assortment of sarcophagi. The severe-looking mosque by the side of the site dates back to the 14th century. It is well worth wandering through Behramkale to admire the fine old Ottoman bridge, built with stone from the ancient site, and the pretty harbour. There are hotels to suit most budgets, and an overnight stay is worth considering. The beach is pebbly but clean.

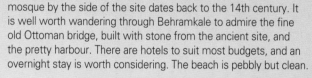

🔲 B5 ✉ 75km (46.5 miles) south of Çanakkale, off the main Çanakkale–Edremit road, next to the village of Behramkale 🕐 Summer daily 8–8; winter daily 8–5 ✋ Inexpensive 🍴 Hotel restaurants (£–££) in Behramkale 🚌 *Dolmuş*/minibus from Ayvacık (not to be confused with Ayvalık further south)

AYDIN

Known in ancient times as Tralles, Aydın today is a busy provincial town with little of intrinsic interest. It is a useful transport point, however, if you want to catch a *dolmuş* east to Nyssa or south to Alinda. If you have time to spare it is worth taking a look in the small archaeology and ethnology museum, west of the park and square that forms the centre of town. Also near the park is an interesting 17th-century mosque. The bus station is over 0.5km (0.3 miles) south of the town centre, just off the main road.

🔲 F10 ✉ 50km (31 miles) east of Kuşadası 🍴 Restaurants (£)
🚌 *Dolmuş*/minibus from Kuşadası, Pamukkale, Selçuk and İzmir
ℹ Just east of the bus station ☎ 0256 614 1103 🕐 Daily 8:30–5

AYVALIK

Ottoman Greeks founded Ayvalık in the 16th century and it was soon the most important town on the coast after İzmir, but after the War of Independence the Greek population was sent to Greece in exchange for Muslims from Lesbos (Lésvos) and Crete. The town's mosques are mostly Greek Orthodox churches with minarets added on, and a stroll takes you past fine examples of domestic Ottoman architecture. A causeway leads to the island of Alibey, which has fish restaurants, but it is best to go there on one of the boats which regularly depart from the quayside. The dock for boats to and from the Greek island of Lesbos is close by, a little to the north. The hotels are all in the nearby beach resort of Sarimsaklı.

🔒 C5 ✉ About halfway between Çanakkale and İzmir 🍴 Restaurants (£–££)
🚌 *Dolmuş*/minibus from Çanakkale, Assos, Bergama and İzmir
ℹ️ On quayside ☎ 0266 312 2122 🕐 May to mid-Oct daily 9–1, 2–7

BERGAMA

Bergama covers part of the glorious ancient city of Pergamum: the lofty acropolis rises at one end of the town, and the Asklepeion lies at the other (➤ 50–51).

Bergama itself is a market town where a donkey and cart is as likely to run you over as one of the tour buses bringing visitors to Pergamum. The archaeological and enthographic museum is not far from the tourist office, and has a very good collection of statuary from Pergamum. The Kızıl Avlu (Red Basilica), at the bottom of the acropolis, was originally a pagan temple, but was converted to a basilica by the Byzantines.

🔒 D6 ✉ 100km (62 miles) north of İzmir, 50km (31 miles) southeast of Ayvalık 🍴 Sağlam (£–££, ➤ 121) 🚌 Buses from Ayvalık and İzmir

🏛 Hükümet Konağı, Zemin Kat, Atatürk Meydanı ☎ 0232 631 2851 🕐 Summer daily 8:30–7; winter Mon–Fri 8:30–12, 1–5

BOZCAADA

According to Homer, the Greeks hid their fleet at Bozcaada while waiting for the Trojans to take the wooden horse into Troy (▶ 116–117). The island is only 5km (3 miles) wide, has no resort hotels and some fine beaches along the south coast.

Near where boats dock are the ruins of a vast, originally Byzantine, castle (open Apr–Nov daily 8–5). The traditional architecture in the island's only town has been well preserved, and there are several *pansiyons* (pensions).

✚ A4 ✉ Just off the coast, south of Truva (Troy), 60km (37 miles) southwest of Çanakkale 🍴 Restaurants (£) near quayside ⛴ Ferry from Yükyeri İskelesi (*dolmuş*/ minibus from Çanakkale)

ÇANAKKALE

Çanakkale lies between East and West, overlooking the narrow Dardanelles strait (► opposite), with Gelibolu (Gallipoli) on the far side and Truva (Troy) just to the south. The place breathes history and mythology, and this romantic atmosphere is enhanced by the coming and going of boats at the docks. Boats also leave for Gökçeada. The docks are the nucleus of the town, and near them are all the hotels and restaurants and the tourist office. A small bazaar area lies inland between the park and the main dock. The formidable Ottoman castle is now a military museum and there are great views from here. A couple of kilometres out of town on the road to Troy is an archaeological museum with a varied collection of artefacts from the region, including Troy.

➕ B3 ✉ 30km (18 miles) northeast of Troy 🍴 Plenty (£–££) 🚍 Buses from Ayvalık, Istanbul, İzmir, Troy ❓ Tours to Gallipoli and Troy

ℹ By the dock ☎ 0286 217 1187

ÇANAKKALE BOĞAZİ (DARDANELLES)

The sea lane that connects the Aegean with the Sea of Marmara has had strategic significance for thousands of years, and has played a crucial part in history and mythology. It was seen as the dividing line between Asia and Europe when the Persian army under Xerxes crossed it on the way to invade Greece in 480BC, and it is still the dividing line today. In 1915 the British and French fleets tried to push through the Dardanelles and capture Istanbul, but failed disastrously (➤ 94–95). In Greek mythology, a woman called Helle fell into the water while fleeing from her mother-in-law and drowned – hence the strait's ancient name of 'Hellespont' (Helle's Sea). In another Greek tale, Leander would swim across to meet his lover, Hero, a priestess of Venus, on the European side. When he was drowned one night, the heartbroken Hero drowned herself too. The poet Byron swam across the Hellespont in 1810.

✚ C2 ▯▯ Restaurants (£–££) in Çanakkale overlooking Çanakkale Boğazi
🚌 Buses from Ayvalık, Istanbul, İzmir, Troy ❓ Tours to Gallipoli from Çanakkale start with a ferry journey across the Dardanelles
ℹ️ İskele Meydanı 67, Çanakkale ☎ 0286 217 1187 🕒 Summer daily 8:30–7; winter daily 8:30–12:30, 1:30–5:30

ÇANDARLI

This small fishing village emerges from hibernation to become a low-key resort between April and October. Çandarlı, site of ancient Pitane, is a place to relax in and enjoy sea walks along the coarse-sand beach and unhurried meals at one of the seafood restaurants. The atmosphere is laid-back, but inviting. A well-preserved 14th-century Genoese castle, although not open to the public, lends character. The liveliest time to visit is on a Friday, when there is a market.

✚ C6 ✉ 40km (25 miles) southwest of Bergama ▯▯ Restaurants and cafés (£–££) along the seafront 🚌 Bus from İzmir

a drive from Çanakkale to Bursa

This is a long drive and you will need to stay overnight in the spa town of Bursa (treatments available). If you want to return to Çanakkale instead, turn back after visiting the Kuşcenneti Milliparkı (National Park).

The E90 connects Çanakkale with Bursa. The first 45km (28 miles) will take you gently up and down hills to beyond the village of Lâpseki (ancient Lampsacus, the traditional birthplace of the phallic god Priapus). There are occasional views of the Dardanelles on the left. Then the road moves inland for about 70km (43 miles), returning to the coast at Denizkent. Some 35km (22 miles) later, you will reach the town of Bandırma.

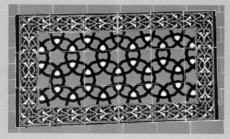

From Bandırma follow the road to Balıkesir for 13km (8 miles) and look for a sign on the right pointing the 5km (3 miles) to the Kuşcenneti National Park (▶ 105). After visiting the park, return to the main road and turn right back on to the E90. Just under 40km (25 miles) before Bursa, look for a

sign pointing right for the fishing village of Gölyazı, 6km (4 miles) from the main road.

Gölyazı is situated by the side of a lake, Uluabat Gölü, and is built over the ruins of ancient Apollonia. Old city walls and a large deserted Greek church are the main points of interest, besides the pleasant scenes of everyday life in a Turkish fishing village.

Return to the main road and complete the journey to Bursa.

Park near the tourist office, in the town centre, and collect a town map and brochure before going to explore the Ottoman houses and other monuments of the city.

Distance 340km (211 miles) (200km (124 miles) to/from Kuşcenneti National Park)
Time 8–10 hours
Start point Çanakkale ✚ B3
End point Bursa ✚ F2 (off map)
Lunch Apollonia Restaurant (£)
✉ North end of the village of Gölyazı

ÇEŞME
Best places to see, ➤ 40–41.

CHRYSE
All that remains of Chryse is the ruined Temple of Apollo
Smintheon, signposted in the village of Gülpinar, but it is a place of
significance in Homer's account of the Trojan War. It was from
here that the Greek leader Agamemnon took Chryseis, the
daughter of the priest of Apollo, for a mistress. He later grudgingly
returned her, to appease Apollo, but only after demanding the
mistress of Achilles as compensation and causing a major row in
the process.

This is the place to read Book I of Homer's *Iliad*, and the
landscape makes the journey from Assos very pleasant. The road
continues west to Babakale, passing a turning on the way to a
lovely beach at Akliman.

➕ B4 ✉ Gülpinar, 20km (12.5 miles) west of Assos 🏛 Free 🍴 Restaurants
(£) in Babakale 🚌 Occasional *dolmuş*/minibus from Assos

DİLEK MİLLİPARKI
This national park covers a large area of mountains, marsh and
beaches, but some parts are used by the military and access to
these is strictly prohibited. What remains open, however, is amply
rewarding for anyone seeking fresh air and a break from ancient
temples or busy resorts.

From the park's entrance it is about 10km (6 miles) to the last
of the pebbly but pretty beaches along the way. The last beach,
Karasu, makes a particularly pleasant spot for a picnic. In the
higher areas, you should catch sight of birds of prey. The
marshes of the Menderes River delta in the southern sector
have waterbirds.

➕ D10 ✉ 28km (17 miles) south of Kuşadası ☎ 0256 646 1079 🕐 Daily
9–8 🏛 Inexpensive 🍴 Snack bars (£) on beaches 🚌 *Dolmuş*/minibus
from Kuşadası

EFES (EPHESUS)

Ephesus was the capital of the Roman province of Asia Minor. It was a major political and cultural centre, and the Romans spared no expense in making this a showcase city for their civilization. It has been very well preserved and is one of the major ancient sites around the Mediterranean. Long before the Romans, Ephesus was home to the cult of Cybele, a mother-goddess. Cybele merged easily with the Greek goddess Artemis, worshipped by the Athenian colonizers who founded a settlement here around 1000BC. Ephesus flourished under Rome and was abandoned only in the sixth century AD after the harbour had silted up.

At least half a day is needed to explore the city (see the Efes walk, ➤ 64–65). You can join a guided tour, although a guide is not essential because the site is compact and there are many specialist guidebooks at the entrance, in the Selçuk tourist office or in the bookshop across the road from it. The highlights include the theatre (➤ 42–43) and the Library of Celsus.

The scant remains of the Temple of Artemis, one of the Seven Wonders of the Ancient World, are passed on the walk from Selçuk to the entrance (signposted as the Artemision, on the left side of the road).

The Library of Celsus, built between AD110 and 135, is an impressive and beautiful structure. The four niches on the two-storeyed facade are filled with plaster copies of the statues of the Four Virtues – Goodness, Thought, Knowledge and Wisdom – whose originals now reside in Vienna.

Beyond the three-arched gateway on the north (right) side is the main *agora* (marketplace – note that it may be off-limits to visitors). Graffiti, both ancient and modern, adorns the walls of the gateway. One inscription in Greek praises the work of a food inspector in fixing the price of bread sold in the *agora*. The library could hold some 14,000 book scrolls. Peer through the grill in the front right corner to see the metre-wide cavity that protected them from winter damp.

The marbled street that runs uphill from the Library of Celsus (➤ 64), Curetes Street, is the main commercial thoroughfare, with rows of shops flanking the stone pavement. The Temple of Hadrian on the left, with its distinctive ornate curved arches, was erected in AD128 to commemorate a visit to the city by the Emperor. The interior arch supports a bas-relief depicting the Tyche goddess of victory.

Behind the streetfronts on both sides of Curetes Street are residential districts, most off-limits to visitors. However, one area on the Bilbul hill slope has

undergone renovation and reveals its many secrets to the public. There's a separate entrance fee to visit the mansions, or Terrace Houses, but it's worth the fee to stand within the domestic spaces once occupied by the wealthier residents of the city.

At the top of the marbled street, one relief is all that remains of the Gate of Hercules. Here the road branches to the right for the Temple of Domitian, one of Rome's more insane emperors (AD81–96). The left route leads past a temple, and on to an odeon, a 1,400-seat theatre, which has been restored. If you are in need of a shady corner, the theatre serves well as a picnic site.

✚ D10 ✉ 3km (2 miles) from Selçuk tourist office ☎ 0232 892 6495 ⏱ Daily 8–5:30. Terrace Houses: daily 8:30–5 ✋ Moderate, with additional charge for Terrace Houses (moderate) 🍴 Restaurants (£–££; not recommended) at the Lower Entrance. Bring a picnic or eat in Selçuk (➤ 125) 🚌 Buses to Selçuk from Kuşadası and İzmir

EFES (EPHESUS) THEATRE

Best places to see, ➤ 42–43.

FOÇA

Nowadays a summer haunt of İzmir's well-to-do, the twin villages of Eski Foça and Yeni Foça (Old and New) were founded in ancient times by Greek colonists who called their colony Phocaea. The Phoceans were famed seafarers, and are credited with founding Massilia (Marseilles). Apart from a fourth century BC tomb, Taş Kule, there is precious little left of the ancient city, but it is a pretty place with some fish restaurants.

✚ C7 ✉ 70km (43 miles) northwest of İzmir 🍴 Restaurants (£–££) 🚌 Bus from İzmir

ℹ Atatürk Bulvarı, just north of central square ☎ 0232 812 5534

GELİBOLU (GALLIPOLI)

Gelibolu, a pretty town on the narrow peninsula of land opposite Çanakkale Boğazı (Dardanelles), is synonymous with a momentous battle of World War I. When the French and British fleets failed to force their way through the Dardanelles (▶ 85), Winston Churchill ordered a troop landing to knock out the Turkish troops guarding the strait. The aim was to secure the Dardanelles, take Istanbul, and organize logistical support for their Russian allies through the Black Sea, but the plan failed in the face of furious Turkish resistance. Thousands of Allied soldiers, including many from the Australia and New Zealand Army Corps (ANZACS), were killed and over 55,000 Turks lost their lives in one of the worst battles of the war. There are organized tours of the battlefield sites and memorials from Çanakkale. One well-established tour company is Hassle Free Travel Agency (tel: 0286 213 5969; www.anzachouse.com). Start at the **Kabatepe Military Museum** in the centre of the peninsula and pick up a leaflet that will guide you around the various landing beaches, memorials and cemeteries. Allow plenty of time. You will need your

own transport if you do not join an organized tour, because the sites are spread out across a wide area.

🚹 C2 ✉ 35km-long (22-mile) peninsula opposite Çanakkale 🕐 Sites are open 24 hours 🍴 Restaurants (£–££) in Gelibolu 🚌 Passenger and vehicle ferry from Çanakkale, or join a tour ❓ Tours available

Kabatepe Military Museum

☎ 0283 814 1297 👋 Inexpensive 🕐 Daily 9–6

GÖKÇEADA

The larger of Turkey's two islands close to Çanakkale Boğazı (Dardanelles) in the North Aegean (the other is Bozcaada, ➤ 83), Gökçeada has the open prison from which William Hayes, of *Midnight Express* fame, escaped. You will need your own transport to reach the island's small villages. There is a pleasant beach on the north coast at Kaleköy, which can also be reached by *dolmuş*.

🚹 A3 ✉ 30km (19 miles) west of Çanakkale 🍴 Fish restaurants (£) 🚌 Ferry from Çanakkale

HERAKLEIA

Originally part of the ancient kingdom of Caria, Herakleıa was fortified and Hellenized in the fourth century BC. The signposted sites are spread out, around and in the small village of Kapıkırı. A good place to start is at the Sanctuary of Endymion. As you walk towards the road from the sanctuary, a sign points to Carian rock tombs on the right. To see them, clamber over the wall and head for the remains of a Byzantine castle on the headland. From the rocks on the other side of the castle walls you can look down on the Carian coffins cut out of the rock.

🚹 K14 ✉ In the village of Kapıkırı 🕐 Open access at all times 👋 Inexpensive, but if ticket office not manned, access is generally free 🍴 Restaurants (£) 🚌 *Dolmuş*/minibus from Çamiçi or boat across Lake Bafa

HIERAPOLIS

Best places to see, ➤ 44–45.

İZMIR (SMYRNA)

The third largest city in Turkey, home to nearly three million people and twinned with Cuba's Havana, İzmir has a long and illustrious past. Homer is said to have lived here in the ninth century BC. The town was destroyed by the Lydians and lay in ruins for over 300 years, but it came back to life when Alexander the Great founded a new city on the summit of Mount Pagus.

Modern İzmir's heyday was in the 19th century when the city was both a major trading port and a cosmopolitan meeting place for merchants from the East and West. It became the focal point of the Greek–Turkish struggle in the War of Independence that followed World War I. When the Turkish army took the city in 1922 the Greek area was set on fire and three-quarters of İzmir burned to the ground. What you see today is a very modern metropolis, with a very Turkish bazaar that should not be missed (➤ 69). Two museums give a good introduction to the city's

ancient and more recent past (➤ 98). Another tangible reminder of the past is Mount Pagus, where Alexander the Great was resting after a hunt when a goddess descended and urged him to found a new city. From the top of the hill there is a dramatic view of the city and the great sweep of a bay that continues to make İzmir the major port on the Aegean.

www.izmirturizm.gov tr

🛉 D8

🛈 Kultur ve Turizm İl Müdürlügü, Akdeniz Mah ✉ 1344 Sok No 2, Pasaport, İzmir ☎ 0232 483 6216/5117

Agora

The Roman *agora* (marketplace) was built by Emperor Marcus Aurelius, after an earthquake in AD178 had destroyed the original one founded by Alexander the Great. A Corinthian colonnade is the main focus of interest, and items discovered here are on display in the Archaeological Museum (➤ 98).

🛉 *İzmir c5* ✉ 816 Sokak ☎ 0232 425 5354 ⏰ Summer daily 8:30–5:30; winter daily 9–12, 1–5 ✋ Inexpensive

Arkeoloji Müzesi (Archaeological Museum)

Greek and Roman statues, monuments and parts of friezes found in and around İzmir fill this excellent purpose-built museum. There are large examples of Roman funerary monuments downstairs, but the more interesting pieces of art are on the ground and upper levels. The examples of Greek archaic art include a fine *kore* (a maiden), while Hellenistic art is represented by a statue of Eros, the god of love.

🔳 *İzmir a6* 🖂 Bahri Baba Park ☎ 0232 489 0796 🕐 Tue–Sat 8:30–5:30
👐 Inexpensive 🍴 Café (£) in the museum

Etnografya Müzesi (Ethnographic Museum)

The first floor includes examples of domestic Ottoman architecture, a reconstructed old pharmacy, exhibits on the art of camel-wrestling and rope-making and a display on the making of blue beads for warding off the evil eye. These beads are usually sold in jewellery shops and are found attached to pendants, chains and even keyrings. The second floor has a reconstructed Ottoman bridal chamber, a 19th-century living room, a circumcision room, and displays of carpets and weapons.

🔳 *İzmir a6* 🖂 Bahri Baba Park ☎ 0232 489 0796 🕐 Tue–Sat 8:30–5:30
👐 Inexpensive

Konak

This central square near the seafront is the most attractive corner of the city. It has an elaborate Ottoman-style clock tower (Saat Kulesi), which was presented to the city in 1901 by the Sultan, and opposite stands a delightful little mosque, enlivened by ornate enamelled tiles. İzmir's two main museums (► above) are just a short distance up the hill in Bahri Baba Park, and the lively bazaar (► 69) is also close by.

🔳 *İzmir a5* 👐 Free ❓ Bazaar closed Sun

a walk around Old İzmir

Start in Cumhuriyet Meydanı, on the waterfront near the statue of Atatürk.

Walk along the seafront to the tourist office for a town map. Continue along to the Pier. Turn left into Fevzipaşa Bulvarı and walk up to the next main junction with Gazi Osmanpaşa where there is a white-on-brown sign for the Agora (➤ 97). There is a small police station on the corner. From the Agora, return to the main road and cross at the traffic lights, walking straight on into Anafartalar Caddesi.

This is the main artery running through İzmir's bazaar (➤ 69). There are side streets to explore, and it is easy to lose your sense of direction among the crowds.

Stay on Anafartalar Caddesi, which bears left after 200m (220yds), and walk down it for about five minutes. Pass by a new mosque on the right, then a dilapidated-looking one on the same side. The road bears left here again and leads into the plaza-like square of Konak (➤ 98). Turn left into the square and walk to the end, past the AKM department store.

At the end of this square you'll eventually find yourself at İzmir's two best museums (➤ 98).

You can reach the top of Mount Pagus from here by taking the No 33 bus to Kadifekale.

Distance 5km (3 miles)
Time 3–4 hours, depending on museum visits and shopping
Start point Cumhuriyet Meydanı ✠ *İzmir b4*
🚌 63, 114, 118 (from train station); 53, 61, 257 (from bus station)
End point Konak bus station ✠ *İzmir a6 (off map)*
Lunch Rihtim Café (£–££) ✉ Atatürk Caddesi 19 at Konak Pier
☎ 0232 446 4751

KUŞADASI

This is one of the major resorts on the Aegean coast and unashamedly proclaimed as such by the scores of carpet shops, jewellers and leatherware stores that fill the town centre. The large harbour, which in summer receives half a dozen huge cruise ships each day, faces Sámos, and the 2km (1-mile) trip to the Greek island is a popular diversion for people staying in Kuşadası. It offers a wide range of entertainment in addition to shopping. At night the pubs, discos, Turkish baths and restaurants are bursting at the seams with happy holidaymakers determined to have a good time. During the day, water-based activities are very popular, and most of the big hotels are able to offer a wide range of sports.

Kuşadası is so dedicated to hedonism that the lack of places of interest within the town itself hardly matters; the most interesting site is the small Bird Island, connected to the mainland by a 400m (440yd) causeway and home to a 16th-century Genoese fortress, which now houses a number of cafés. Kuşadası is well placed, however, for visits to many of the Turkish Aegean's most extraordinary ancient sites. Ephesus is a short bus ride away, and the ancient Greek settlements of Milet (Miletus), Didim (Didyma) and Priene may be easily visited by public transport or on a three-in-a-day guided tour. Afrodisias, Pamukkale and Hierapolis are a couple of hours away by road.

The main esplanade, Atatürk Bulvarı, runs past the harbour where boats to and from Sámos dock. The nearby Öküz Mehmet Pasa Kervansaray (now a noisy hotel) is a useful landmark in this town, which has no obvious centre. At the junction of the hotel and the esplanade, a pedestrianized street, Barbaros Hayrettin Bulvarı, runs inland. To the left, as you ascend this street, lies the old part of town, known as Kale, where some picturesque buildings have been converted into clubs, bars and restaurants.

Kadinlar Plaji (Ladies Beach), 3km (2 miles) southwest of town and easily reached by minibus, has a cluster of resort hotels and is very well known, but the cleaner pools of nearby hotels may seem more inviting. A better choice is Tusan Beach, 5km (3 miles) from the other side of town on the road to Selçuk and also easily reached by minibus.

Moderately priced accommodation is available near the town centre; the 4- and 5-star hotels are stretched out in bunches along the coastline at either end of town, but they are nearly all easily reached by minibuses from the seafront road. These minibuses will usually stop opposite the main bus station, which is outside town on the main İzmir–Söke road. This can be an uncomfortably long walk in summer, but to get to Söke (the major local transport hub and the departure point for buses to places of historical interest) there is an unofficial minibus meeting point nearer to the centre of town, and most of the hotel minibuses also stop here.

www.kusadasi.com

🕇 D10 ✉ 95km (59 miles) south of İzmir, 20km (12.5 miles) south of Ephesus
🍴 Restaurants (£–£££) 🚌 *Dolmuş*/minibus from Bodrum, İzmir, Pamukkale, Selçuk and Söke

🛈 Liman Caddesi ☎ 0256 614 1103 ⏰ May–Sep daily 8–6; Oct–Apr daily 8–12, 1:30–5:30

KUŞCENNETİ MİLLİPARKI (NATIONAL PARK)

This bird sanctuary, whose name translates as 'Bird Paradise', lies between Çanakkale and Bursa (➤ 86–87). An exhibit inside the entrance shows what birds may be seen from the nearby observation post (bring your own binoculars). Herons, cormorants, pelicans and spoonbills frequent the reserve and you may see the occasional spotted eagle. From April to June and September to November are the best times to visit because so many species migrate at these times. Over 250 different species have been identified.

✚ F3 ✉ 20km (12.5 miles) south of Bandırma ⏰ Daily 7–5:30
✋ Inexpensive 🚌 Bus from Çanakkale

a drive around ancient Caria

This drive leaves the hustle and bustle of Kuşadası to explore the ancient kingdom of Caria, taking in Bafa Gölü (Lake Bafa) and a number of interesting Hellenic sites, some of which are difficult to reach without your own transport.

From Kuşadası take the road to Söke (515) and when it meets the main İzmir–Milas road, the 525, turn right, signposted for Milas, and head south. Once the road starts to hug the shores of Lake Bafa, park by one of the lake-side restaurants.

It is possible to take a swim in the lake, and there are passenger boats to Herakleıa (► 95). This drive takes you to Herakleıa by road.

Drive on about 6km (4 miles) to the village of Çamiçi and take the road signposted left to Herakleıa. After visiting Herakleıa, return to Çamiçi and turn left to continue towards Milas for about 15km (9 miles). Look for a signpost on the left to Euromos (► 154), 1km (0.5 miles) south of Selimiye.

After visiting Euromos, continue for another 12km (7.5 miles) and turn left at the sign for Kargicak if you wish to make the 14km (9-mile) detour to Labranda (► 164). The road is narrow, with tarmac washed away on both sides and plenty of low gear shifting will be needed to make the steep ascent.

Return to the main road. If time permits, it is only a few kilometres further on to Milas (► 169). Otherwise, turn right when meeting the main road from Kargicak and return to Kuşadası.

Distance 178km (110 miles)
Time 4–6 hours, depending on length of stops
Start/end point Kuşadası ✚ D10
Lunch Zeybek or Agora restaurant (£)

MAGNESIA ON THE MAEANDER

Homesick colonists from Magnesia in Greece founded this ancient
city and it was presented to the Athenian soldier and statesman
Themistocles by a Persian king. He is said to have committed
suicide here. It requires some imagination to make sense of the
scattered remains of this temple but it is likely you'll have the
place to yourself, which gives it a certain charm.

➕ E10 ✉ 16km (10 miles) north of Söke 🕐 Daily 8:30–5:30 ✋ Inexpensive
🚌 *Dolmuş*/minibus from Söke and Selçuk

MANİSA

Founded in the aftermath of the fall of Troy and destroyed by
Greeks soldiers retreating in 1922, contemporary Manisa is a
modern town with a commercial air, redeemed by a grand
backdrop of mountains and a city centre worth a half-day's
exploration. The tourist office is in the centre of town and you can
pick up a map and brochure there before setting out to visit the
three 16th-century mosques and a small museum with material
from Sart (Sardis, ➤ 113).

➕ E7 ✉ 40km (25 miles) northeast of İzmir 🍴 Restaurants (£) 🚌 Buses
from İzmir, Sart or Salihli; train from İzmir

ℹ️ Anafartalar Mah 1 MKP Cad ☎ 0236 232 3347 🕐 Mon–Sat 8–12, 1–5

MERYEMANA

The story that the Virgin Mary came to Ephesus with St Paul
gained credibility in the early 19th century, when a German nun
who had never been to Turkey described a vision of the house
where Mary stayed. A priest in İzmir matched the description with
a chapel just south of Ephesus. Sanctioned by a papal visit in
1967, Meryemana is now regarded as the place where Mary lived
out her last years, and receives a steady stream of pilgrims.

➕ D10 ✉ 8km (5 miles) south of Ephesus ☎ 0232 892 1328 (Selçuk Tourist
Office) 🕐 Dawn–dusk ✋ Inexpensive to site; churches free
🍴 Café (£) near entrance 🚌 Taxi from Selçuk

MİLET (MILETUS)

By far the most important of the Greek colonies established along the Aegean coast, Miletus was originally on an inlet of the sea, but a marshy delta, much loved by frogs, has now formed around the site. The remains you see today belong to the city recreated after a destructive onslaught by the Persians in 495BC. When a play on the Persian defeat of Miletus was performed in ancient Athens the audience burst into tears and the playwright was fined for causing such dismay.

The large theatre is a good vantage point to view the site, which was laid out in a grid pattern (still visible). Parts of a *nymphaeum* (fountain), *agora* (marketplace) and Roman baths survive.

✚ K14 ✉ 22km (14 miles) south of Priene
☎ No phone ⏱ Daily 8–5
✋ Inexpensive
🍴 Overpriced snack bars (££) near the entrance
🚌 *Dolmuş*/minibus from Söke ❓ Tours from Kuşadası combine Miletus, Priene and Didyma

NOTİON AND KLAROS

Notion was a typically small ancient Greek settlement, and although very little remains today, the site is attractively located and offers a fine view of the sea. Signposts lead from Notion to the site of ancient Klaros just over 1km (0.5 miles) away. Never a city, Klaros was famed for its temple and oracle of Apollo (undergoing excavation and restoration), whose priest was able to answer the needs of those making a consultation without ever hearing their question. The source of inspiration was a sacred spring and parts of the underground chamber enclosing it can be clearly made out.

➕ D6 ✉ 25km (22 miles) north of Kuşadası ⏰ Dawn–dusk 💷 Free
🚌 *Dolmuş*/minibus from Kuşadası to Seferihisar. Ask for Notion

NYSSA

Many of Turkey's minor ancient Greek and Roman sites have attractive settings, and Nyssa's is especially so. The city was founded in the third century BC and flourished well into Roman times. Strabo, a geographer of the first century BC, described it as a 'double city', and there are some remains of two bridges that linked the settlement across a tumultuous stream. A theatre and semi-circular *bouleuterion* (meeting hall) are the main sights; the long tunnel that the citizens built to help drain the city can also be made out.

Nyssa is not visited by tour buses, but it is easy to reach by car or public transport and, like Notion and Klaros (➤ above), makes a good day trip from Kuşadası (➤ 102–105).

➕ M13 ✉ 2km (1.2 miles) from Sultanhisar, 14km (9 miles) west of Nazilli
⏰ Daily 8:30–5:30 💷 Inexpensive 🍴 Restaurants (£) in Sultanhisar
🚌 Buses between Kuşadası and Denizli will stop at Sultanhisar

PAMUKKALE

Best places to see, ➤ 48–49.

PERGAMUM

Best places to see, ➤ 50–51.

PRIENE

Ancient Priene, founded around the 11th century BC, now lies under the alluvial plain, but the city that developed from the fourth century BC high on the mountain above is in remarkably good shape. It never attracted much attention from the Romans, and the happy result is a Hellenistic city uncluttered by Roman or Byzantine additions and modifications. The theatre should not be missed: the front row has five marble thrones for special guests, and faces the Altar of Dionysus, where a sacrifice began the day's entertainment. The two-storey stage and its projecting proscenium have, to a remarkable degree, weathered the last 2,000 years, and the holes and sockets for decorated wooden panels may be seen clearly on some of the front pillars which held up the stage.

The Temple of Athena Polias was regarded in ancient times as the epitome of Ionic temple architecture. When English archaeologists arrived in the 1860s the temple walls were still standing at over 1.5m (5ft) in places. To the north of the temple lie the scant remains of a sanctuary to Demeter and Kore; far more substantial are the remains of the *bouleuterion* (meeting hall) to the south of the theatre. The gymnasium and small stadium, on the south, lower front side of the site, are worth seeking out. Some of the starting blocks for foot races can still be made out. It's a steep walk up to the site from the car park, but the setting is truly stunning. Remember to take water.

🔲 D10 ✉ 35km (22 miles) south of Kuşadası ☎ 0256 547 1165 🕐 Daily
8:30–sunset 🖐 Inexpensive 🍴 Restaurants (£) in adjoining village of
Güllübahçe 🚌 *Dolmuş*/minibus from Söke ❓ Tours from Kuşadası combine
Priene, Miletus and Didyma

SART (SARDIS)

There are two main sites at Sart: the Greek Temple of Artemis and
the Roman city of the fifth century AD. The wonderful Temple of
Artemis is signposted on the right, as you come from İzmir, and
is reached after a 1km (0.5-mile) walk. The setting is idyllic,
surrounded by pinnacles of rock, with the occasional tinkling of
sheep bells in the background as a shepherd moves his flock.
Although only two columns remain completely upright, there is
plenty to inspire the imagination. An Ionic capital, resting in front of
a rusting excavator's crane, is reputed to be one of the best
examples you are likely see at such close quarters. The Roman
town has been excavated and restored.

🔲 F8 ✉ 100km (60 miles) east of İzmir 🕐 Daily 8:30–5:30, closes for lunch
in winter 🖐 Inexpensive 🍴 Two *köfte* restaurants (£–££) in Salihli (9km/5.5
miles) 🚌 Bus from İzmir

SELÇUK

The tourist industry in this small town is entirely due to its proximity to Ephesus. It makes an ideal place for a short stay because it is also close to the ancient sites south of Kuşadası. The Ephesus Museum displays finds from Ephesus: do not miss the Artemis Room, with its many-breasted statue of the goddess. The adjoining ethnographic section is also recommended. The Hill of Ayasoluk towers over the town, with Byzantine-Turkish fortifications and the remains of St John's Basilica, built to mark the final resting place of St John the Evangelist. From Selçuk you can make a pleasant day trip to the old Greek town of Şirince, only 8km (5 miles) away.

www.selcuk.gov.tr

✚ D10 ✉ 20km (12.5 miles) northeast of Kuşadası 🍴 Restaurants (£–££)
🚌 Bus from İzmir, *dolmuş*/minibus from Kuşadası
ℹ Atatürk Mah ☎ 0232 892 1328 🕙 Mon–Fri 8:30–5:30, Sat, Sun 9–5 in summer

SİĞACIK AND TEOS

The lack of a sandy beach ensures that Siğacık, a village that has grown up inside the walls of a Genoese fortress, remains a low-key destination. Just 1.5km (1 mile) away, however, the beach at Akkum is a developing resort that is steadily and relentlessly encroaching on Siğacık. The site of ancient Teos, 5km (3 miles) from Siğacık, is the best reason for visiting this stretch of coastline between İzmir and Çeşme. Travel author Freya Stark wrote: 'It is where I should live, if I had the choice of all the cities of Ionia.' The city was the birthplace of the lyric poet Anakreon (c540BC) and was a renowned centre for the cult of Dionysus, a Greek nature god of vegetation and fruitfulness, particularly associated with wine and ecstacy. The remains of a Temple of Dionysus, once the largest in the ancient world, are the ruined site's main attraction.

✚ C9 ✉ 40km (25 miles) southwest of İzmir 🕙 Open 24 hours ✋ Free
🍴 Restaurants (£) in Siğacık 🚌 *Dolmuş*/minibus from İzmir

TRUVA (TROY)

Troy was thought to have existed only in Homer's imagination until excavations began in 1870, financed by the German businessman Heinrich Schliemann, who was obsessed with finding the historic city. He discovered not one but four settlements, built over the ruins of each other, and later excavations suggest that there were nine main periods of occupation. The first five, known as Troy I to Troy V (3000–1800BC), follow a similar cultural pattern, but a change then occurs, as prosperity grew from maritime trading links in the Aegean and the Black Sea. This could have brought conflict with the Greeks, who besiege Troy in Homer's *Iliad*. The epic poem tells a highly charged tale of war, love and honour, aided and hindered by the pantheon of Greek gods. It was enormously influential not only for the ancient Greeks, but for later European civilization itself.

Homer's Troy may have been Troy VI (1800–1275BC), which was destroyed either by an earthquake in 1275BC or by being stormed and set on fire (or both, over time). Settlements of the site went on into Roman times, with Troy IX (300BC–AD300)

completing the saga. The enormous wooden horse at the entrance to Troy leaves no doubt as to which of the city's many eras captures the interest of modern visitors.

There is a lot to see, but it is a place of ditches, mounds and fragments rather than great structures. The whole site is surprisingly small, or perhaps only the crowds make it seem so; it is worth turning up early in the morning or as late as possible. When viewed from the city walls, the dismally flat plain that stretches ahead can be evocative of ancient battles and, with only a little imagination, the 300m (330ft) stretch of inward-leaning and curving wall of Troy VI will conjure up images of the scene of Hector being dragged by furious Achilles around the parapets. Inside the city one of the most impressive sights is the massive stone ramp that could have carried the Wooden Horse – except that it belongs to Troy II (2500–2300BC).

✚ B3 ✉ 25km (15.5 miles) south of Çanakkale ☎ 0286 283 0061 🕐 May–Oct daily 8:30–7; Nov–Apr daily 9:30–5 ✋ Moderate, plus charge for parking (inexpensive) 🚌 *Dolmuş*/minibus from Çanakkale ❓ Tours from Çanakkale often include Gallipoli (▶ 94–95)

HOTELS

ASSOS
Assos Kervansaray (££)

One of several small hotels in Behremkale, below Assos, this is a charming stone building, with fine sea views, a pool and restaurant with an outdoor terrace. Boat trips and watersports also available.

✉ Behramkale, Ayvacik ☎ 0286 721 7093/7199;
www.assoskervansaray.com

ÇANAKKALE
Akol (££–£££)

This 4-star hotel at the east end of town is the most comfortable accommodation base for visits to Troy and Gallipoli. The two blocks have a small pool between them. Most of the 136 rooms face the Dardanelles, and there are two restaurants and a roof bar.

✉ Kordonboyu ☎ 0286 217 9456; www.hotelakol.com.tr

Anzac House (£)

Good budget choice. The single, double and dormitory rooms are clean. Facilities include an inexpensive cafeteria, laundry service, Internet, summer barbecues and hot showers. Member of the Turkish Youth Hostels Association.

✉ Cumhuriyet Meydanı 61 ☎ 0286 213 5969; www.anzachouse.com

ÇEŞME
Sheraton Çesme (£££)

A seriously luxurious 5-star resort, about 2km (1.2 miles) from the centre of town, with a private beach, several restaurants, superb food, a rooftop bar, indoor and outdoor pools and a sybaritic spa.

✉ Sifme Caddesi 35, Ilıca ☎ 0232 723 1240; www.sheratoncesme.com

HERAKLEIA
Agora (£)

One of the most pleasant places for an overnight stay amid the evocative remains of ancient Herakleia (the modern village name is Kapıkırı). Simple pine beds, a pleasant veranda and lots of local information. No English but German is spoken.

✉ Kapıkırı ☎ 0252 543 5445 🚌 *Dolmuş*/minibus from Çamiçi or by boat from south shore of Lake Bafa

İZMİR
Antik Han Hotel (£)
One of the city's few 'special' hotels, in a restored historic shopping mall in the middle of the market area. It has a lobby bar, restaurant and shady courtyard garden, a good place to sit out of the heat of the day or escape the bustle beyond the doors. Rooms are unpretentious but then, so is the price.
✉ Anafartalar Caddesi 600, Mezarlıkbası ☎ 0232 489 2750; www.otelantikham.com

KÜCÜKKUYU
Manici Kasri Hotel (£££)
This traditional stone building nestled against a limestone hillside houses one of Turkey's finest boutique hotels. Each individually styled room is furnished with local pieces and lovely handmade carpets. There's a large terrace for dining and two cafés on site.
✉ Yeşilyurt Löyü, Küçükkuyu, Çanakkale ☎ 0286 752 1731; www.manicikasri.com

KUŞADASI
Atinç Otel (££)
Perfectly situated on the seafront, a few minutes' walk from the town centre, the Antiç is a modern 4-star hotel with great sea views, a bar, two good restaurants (one a popular pizzeria) and a rooftop pool. The rooms, which have balconies, are comfortable and the staff are friendly and helpful.
✉ Atatürk Bulvarı ☎ 0256 612 0505; www.atincotel.com

Liman Hotel (£)
Around the corner from the tourist office, the best rooms at the Liman have balconies and face the sea. All rooms have air-conditioning and breakfast is served on the roof. Other facilities include laundry service, Internet, restaurant and bar.
✉ Buyral Sok 4 ☎ 0256 614 7770; www.limanhotel.com

Villa Konak (£–££)

A welcoming 'special' hotel, in a restored mansion in a hilly residential area of the town. The rooms are simply but elegantly furnished. Meals are taken family-style at a huge communal table, and the shady courtyard garden is ideal to relax in.

✉ Yildirim Caddesi 55 ☎ 0256 614 6318; www.villakonakhotel.com

MANİSA
Anemon Manisa (££)

A couple of kilometres outside Manisa, on the road to İzmir, a mountain provides a dramatic backdrop to the hotel. Indoor and outdoor swimming pools, tennis courts and a fitness centre.

✉ Manisa ☎ 0232 233 4141; www.anemonhotels.com

PAMUKKALE
Colossae Hotel Thermal (££)

One of a positive epidemic of upmarket spas that have invaded the plateau behind Pamukkale, the Colossae doubles as a tour-group friendly hotel and health resort. Nicely decorated rooms, gardens, two pools, restaurants and nightclub.

✉ Karahayit ☎ 0258 271 4156; www.colossae.com.tr

SELÇUK
Kalehan (£–££)

The Ottoman charm of the Kalehan, near the castle, on the main road through town, puts it in a class of its own. The rooms are delightfully furnished and comfortably modern. Antiques and artefacts are everywhere and lend character to the place. There is a swimming pool and a good restaurant.

✉ Atatürk Caddesi 49 ☎ 0232 892 6154; www.kalehan.com

ŞIRINCE
Kirkinca Konaklari (£–££)

Set in the pretty village of Sirince, 9km (5.5 miles) from Selçuk, here you can combine the calm of the countryside, traditional Turkish village life and sightseeing in Selçuk and Ephesus.

✉ Şirince ☎ 0232 898 3133; www.kirkinca.com

RESTAURANTS

AYVALIK
Canli Balik (££)
Fish and seafood are the mainstays of the menu at this popular harbourside restaurant. Locals flock for whole fish simply grilled or excellent crispy squid or octopus.

✉ On the harbour, Cumhuriyet Square ☎ 0266 313 0081 🕔 Lunch and dinner 🚌 *Dolmuş*/minibus from Çanakkale, Assos, Bergama and İzmir

BERGAMA
Sağlam (£–££)
On the main street in the centre of town. At lunchtime there are the standard hot dishes waiting in steamtrays, but it's worth asking about the regional dishes from Urfa. There is a small courtyard at the back for alfresco dining, and rooms upstairs.

✉ Cumhuriyet Meydanı 29 ☎ 0232 632 8897 🕔 Daily 8–8

ÇANAKKALE
Yalova (££)
The seafront in Çanakkale is lined with restaurants, but few are worth bothering about. This fish restaurant near the ferry port is the pick of the bunch, with its rooftop terrace and fine views.

✉ Gümrük Sok, Liman Caddesi ☎ 0286 217 1045 🕔 Lunch and dinner

ÇEŞME
Dost Pide & Pizza (£–££)
A bright and cheerful tourist restaurant in Ilıca, 4km (2.5 miles) west of Çeşme, with tables filling the pavement. As well as the pizzas, there is also a variety of meat dishes on the menu.

✉ İifne Caddesi, Ilıca ☎ 0232 723 2059 🕔 Daily 8am–late 🚌 *Dolmuş* to Çeşme

Sahíl (£–££)
This is a typical Çeşme restaurant facing the sea, with indoor and outdoor tables, and a menu that has both Turkish and European dishes, including kebabs and pizza.

✉ Cumhuriyet Meydanı 13 ☎ 0232 712 8294 🕔 Daily 8am–11pm

CUNDA
Lale Restaurant (££–£££)
One of the best known restaurants in northwestern Turkey, Lale is run with efficiency and friendliness by Mr Nihat (it's often called Nihat's place instead of Lale). The freshest seafood is cooked to perfection and there are rare delicacies including local aquades clams. The waterfront setting is delightful for summer dining, but there's a welcoming dining room for the winter.

✉ Waterfront, Cunda Island, off coast near Ayvalık ☎ 0266 327 1777
🕔 Lunch and dinner (closed during Ramadan) ⛴ Ferry from Ayvalık

FOÇA
Celep Restaurant (£)
The atmospheric harbour at Foça has several restaurants, but Celep is most popular with local Turks, hence it must have the best local cuisine. Grilled meats, fish and *meze* dishes are the stars of the menu, and you can watch the strolling crowds in the warm evenings during the summer.

✉ Harbourfront ☎ 0232 812 1495 🕔 Lunch and dinner

GELİBOLU
Yelkençi (££)
This simple harbourfront restaurant offers an excellent range of seafood, including specialities of squid or sardines – fresh and simply cooked with a glass of *raki*, perfect for lunch, dinner or as a snack while you wait for the ferry.

✉ Balikhane ☎ 0286 566 4600 🕔 Lunch and dinner

İZMİR
Chinese Restaurant (££)
Situated down a street behind the Hilton Hotel, this licensed restaurant has a long menu of beef, chicken, duck, seafood, rice and noodle dishes. The cook's specials include a hot cabbage salad, lamb with green onion, fried chicken with orange sauce and steamed dumplings. Take-away service available.

✉ 1379 Sokak ☎ 0232 483 0079 🕔 Lunch and dinner 🚌 62, 68, 77

Deniz (££–£££)

The Deniz specializes in fish dishes, and is regarded as the best fish restaurant in town. You may need to make a reservation to secure one of the outdoor tables. Popular with business people during the week, less formal at weekends.

✉ Atatürk Caddesi 188-B ☎ 0232 422 0601 ⏰ Lunch and dinner

Fish House (££)

One of a number of restaurants lining the waterfront promenade, this is a coolly calm restaurant with crisp white tablecloths and outside tables in summer. The food, particularly the seafood, is excellent.

✉ Atatürk Caddesi 174/1-A, Kordon ☎ 0232 463 1020 ⏰ Lunch and dinner

İzmir Ticaret Odasi Lokali (£)

One of the last few traditional quick lunch spots left in the city, this is a place to try one of Turkey's specialities, tripe soup. It's often eaten after a night out to reenergise partygoers. Less exotic items include tasty kebabs and grilled meats.

✉ Vasif Cinar Bulvarı 1 ☎ 0232 421 4249 ⏰ Mon–Fri lunchl

Window on the Bay (£££)

Open nightly, except Sunday, the Window on the Bay is on the 31st floor of the Hilton Hotel. Nowhere in town offers finer views of the city. An international menu is accompanied by piano music until 10pm, and then a band takes over.

✉ Gaziosmanpasa Bulvarı, İzmir ☎ 0232 441 6060 ⏰ Mon–Sat 7pm–2am
🚌 61–3, 110, 112, 116, 150

KUŞADASI
Captain's House Restaurant (££)

Next door to the pub of the same name, this is a comfortable place to enjoy seafood, international dishes and good Turkish *meze*. Photographs and charts relating to the Turkish navy decorate the walls and just about any other available space.

✉ Istikal ☎ 0256 614 4754 ⏰ Daily 8:30am–late

Ferah Balik Restaurant (££)

Right beside the sea, near the fishing harbour, this is a charmingly laid-back restaurant with excellent seafood, a seafront terrace in summer and fine views of Bird Island.

✉ İskele Yanı ☎ 0256 614 1281 ◷ Lunch, dinner

Gondolen Pizzeria (£)

Small, modern, licensed café with a large menu of over 20 pizzas to choose from as well as other possibilities, including English-style breakfast and a children's menu. A few doors up on the same side of the street, opposite the Otel Atadan, there is a less expensive, unlicensed *pide* (pizza) café specializing in the one dish: a tasty mixed *pide*, with or without meat, accompanied by a Turkish yogurt.

✉ Ismet Inönö Bulvarı 19 ☎ 0256 614 5417 ◷ Daily 8am–late

Güldüoğlu (££–£££)

In the centre of town, close to Beer Street, this is an elegant, air-conditioned restaurant with rosewood furniture and modern art by the painter/proprietor adorning the walls, which is for sale. There's a mixed menu – grills and pasta dishes – in English, Dutch, French, German and Spanish. Some tables outside.

✉ 1/C Zabita Amirliğ, Alti ☎ 0256 614 8637 ◷ Daily 8am–11pm ▣ Free transport to/from hotels

Holiday Inn (£)

In the heart of Kuşadası, and with a wide-ranging menu designed to appeal to overseas visitors: salads, lasagne, kebabs, moussaka, chicken Kiev, roast beef, steaks, fish and chips, Wiener Schnitzel etc. Stick with the home-made kebabs and you won't be disappointed.

✉ Kahramanlar Caddesi 57/5 ☎ 0256 612 8940 ◷ Daily 8am–midnight ▣ Free transport to/from hotels

Planet Yucca Restaurant (££)

Large, very commercial tented restaurant serving almost every cuisine under the sun, from Mexican, Indian and Chinese to

French and Italian – and Turkish, of course. With a shady garden terrace and lively atmosphere and good food, it's the hangout choice for locals.

✉ Soğlik Caddesi 65 ☎ 0256 612 5730 ⏱ Lunch, dinner May–Oct

Sultan Han (£££)

A charming setting in the old part of town; the Sultan Han is in a renovated old caravanserai and some care has been taken to retain a traditional atmosphere. The menu is fairly wide ranging, but the Turkish dishes are definitely the ones to go for. The *meze* are very tasty and there is a good selection of traditional sugary Turkish desserts. Belly dancers sometimes provide live entertainment.

✉ Bahar Sokak 8 ☎ 0256 614 6380/3849 ⏱ Lunch, dinner

SELÇUK

Kalenin Prensin (££)

Attractive gardens, a shaded terrace and an ancient Roman menu alongside the standard Turkish fare to get you in the mood for visiting Ephesus all help to make this one of the more unusual and entertaining restaurants in the area.

✉ İsabey Mahallesi Eski İzmir ☎ 0232 892 2087 ⏱ Lunch, dinner May–Oct

Pink Bistro (£)

The menu here includes hamburgers, spaghetti, kebabs, Turkish pizza and salads. It is not gourmet dining, but it is pleasant enough. Late at night this is a lively bar playing taped music to a European clientele in the 20–30 age group.

✉ Atatürk Mh Saigburg Sokak ☎ 0232 891 4015 ⏱ Daily 9am–2:30am

Selçuk Köftecisi (£–££)

With a reputation among locals as the best place in town for *köfte* (meatballs), this restaurant now occupies a larger space on the road near the bus station, behind the tourist office. Try the *köfte* with a salad and a choice of kebabs, a glass of *raki* and to round off one of the sweet desserts to complete your meal.

✉ Cahabettin Dede Caddesi ☎ 0232 892 6696 ⏱ Summer 7:30am–11pm; winter 7:30am–9pm

SHOPPING

ÇEŞME
Erdal's
Small gifts and souvenirs: crystal, ceramics, brass and copper, onyx, wood carvings, Meerschaum pipes.

✉ 16 Eylül Mh Gümrük Caddesi 21 ☎ 0232 712 6161 🕓 Daily 8:30am–9pm
🚌 *Dolmuş*/minibus to İzmir

İZMİR
Anatolia
High-quality handwoven carpets and *kilims* are sold here. For smaller purchases, expect a discount of at least 15 per cent; for really expensive carpets it should be at least 25 per cent.

✉ 928 Sokak 25 (Hilton Hotel Shopping Mall) ☎ 0232 441 7578
🕓 Mon–Sat 9–9

Mihrap
Handwoven carpets of silk, wool and cotton and a selection of *kilims*. Bargain hard and expect at least 30 per cent off the asking price. Tucked away in a modern little mall in the bazaar.

✉ Kapalicarsi, Anafartalar Caddesi, Konak ☎ 0232 484 0425 🕓 Daily 9am–7pm 🚌 86, 169

KUŞADASI
Albatros
There are lots of places to check prices on and around this street, and Albatros is a good place to start. There are two floors of leather goods: belts, briefcases, backpacks and handbags.

✉ Barbaros Hayrettin Paşa Street ☎ 0256 614 1918 🕓 Daily 9am–late

Asia Shop 2
Best reached by walking up the street behind the tourist office, this store is worth seeking out if you need to buy a lot of small gifts and souvenirs. There are two floors crammed with inexpensive bric-a-brac, and the fixed prices mean you can wander around looking and choosing instead of having to haggle.

✉ Kibris Caddesi 4 ☎ 0256 614 1393 🕓 Daily 7:30am–1am

Çerge

In the winter, Turkish shoppers come here to buy decorative items for their homes, while in summer the shop appeals to visitors looking for something more than an inexpensive souvenir.

✉ Kemal Ankan Caddesi 16 ☎ 0256 612 5821 🕔 Daily 8:30–midnight

Faberce

This easy-to-find store near the entrance to the bazaar has two floors of carpets and *kilims*. Delivery and insurance is arranged for bulky purchases, usually around 2 per cent of the price.

✉ Söförler Sokak 3, Grand Bazaar ☎ 0256 614 8885 🕔 Daily 7:30am–midnight

Galeri Sultan

Claims to be the oldest leather emporium in Kuşadası. A good collection of jackets and some less expensive waistcoats. A family-run shop with a prime location in the Grand Bazaar.

✉ Grand Bazaar 5 ☎ 0256 612 4569 🕔 Daily 7:30am–1am

PRIENE
Onyx Factory and Shop

The workshop and adjoining store are in the corner of the square where the minibuses arrive and depart. Unless the shop is very busy, someone is usually glad to show you around the workshop and explain the process, from the arrival of the uncut stone to its final polishing. Prices are reasonable, and there is a good selection.

✉ Priene ☎ 0256 547 1123 🕔 8am–9pm 🚌 *Dolmuş*/minibus from Söke

SELÇUK
Golden Ephesus Jewellery Centre

A vast jewellery emporium with styles and quality at all prices and enough jewellers on the premises to make up your designs during your stay. Demonstrations of the craft and loose stones for sale.

✉ Aydın Karayolu 3km (2miles), Mersinli Mevkii ☎ 0232 892 9550; www.goldenephesus.com 🕔 Daily 9am–10pm

Nomadic Art Gallery

Come here for expensive, hand-woven wool carpets from Anatolia, less expensive cotton ones and imports from Iran and Afghanistan. It pays to know something about carpets and to be able to distinguish between materials of different quality.

✉ Atatürk Mh Cengiz Topel Caddesi 26/A ☎ 0232 891 8650 🕓 Daily 8am–11pm

TRUVA (TROY)
Ilion Tur

Just outside Troy in the village of Trevfikiye, the usual Troy memorabilia is on sale here. Also on sale are Turkish baggy pants, books on ancient history and assorted souvenirs.

✉ Trevfikiye ☎ 0286 283 0823 🕓 9am–11pm

ENTERTAINMENT

ÇANAKKALE
Akol Roof Bar

The Roof Bar on the top floor of the Akol Hotel (➤ 118) is the best place to enjoy a cocktail while watching the sun set over the Dardanelles. Depending on your taste, the live popular music will either add to or detract from the overall experience.

✉ Akol Hotel, Kordonboyu ☎ 0286 217 9456 🕓 Daily 7am–midnight

ILICA
Beach Grill Restaurant and Terrace

Atmospheric beach bar for late-night cocktails.

✉ Sheraton Çeşme Hotel, Resort and Spa, Sifne Caddesi ☎ 0232 723 1240 🕓 May–Oct daily 5pm–midnight

KUŞADASI
Captain's House Café

A pub and restaurant with a sociable buzz every night, and live music. It's a popular choice with holidaymakers who appreciate the understated Turkish ambience.

✉ Atatürk Caddesi 66 ☎ 0256 612 1200 🕓 Daily 9:30am–late

Bodrum

Contemporary Bodrum is a major resort, but still has a traditional Mediterranean flavour, with whitewashed, flat-roofed homes dotting the terraced hillsides. The opening of an

Bodrum

international airport 40km (25 miles) away has given a fresh boost to its thriving tourist industry, and despite lacking its own beach, Bodrum is the most chic and European resort on Turkey's Aegean coast.

The original name of Bodrum was Halicarnassos and it was founded in the 11th century BC by Greek colonists. Notable inhabitants have included the historian Herodotus (fifth century BC), and Mausolus (377–353BC), who was installed as king after a

Persian invasion. Halicarnassos fell into obscurity during Roman and Byzantine times until the Knights of St John arrived from nearby Rhodes in 1402 and built the massive Castle of St Peter that continues to tower over the town. The word *bodrum* means 'dungeon' or 'underground vault' in Turkish, so its modern name presumably comes from the castle or the mausoleum.

BODRUM

The Castle of St Peter (Bodrum Kalesi) is the obvious landmark and directly in front of it, due north, is the tourist office. The pedestrianized streets to the north of the tourist office make up the town's bazaar and this is the central shopping area for leather, clothes, carpets and assorted souvenirs and gifts. Dr Alim Bey

Caddesi is the main street facing the sea to the east. At the end of the bazaar area the street becomes Cumhuriyet Caddesi, and forms the heart of Bodrum's legendary nightlife. The sea-facing street that follows the harbour's curve to the west of the tourist office, Nezen Tevfik Caddesi, brings you past open-air restaurants and cafés to the marina and the quieter end of town. The main street from the bus station, Cevat İşakir

Caddesi, has more shops, restaurants and the post office.

During the high season Bodrum is definitely not a place for anyone seeking a quiet retreat; the sophisticated nightclubs are the loudest on the coast. The mornings in Bodrum are relatively quiet, but only because so many visitors are sound asleep after carousing and dancing until dawn. The town itself is not overdeveloped, but it acts as a hub for the stream of resorts around the Bodrum peninsula, ensuring the streets are jammed packed.

Bodrum's marina is a favourite destination for yachts cruising the Aegean and Mediterranean, and the town is an ideal place to organize a sailing excursion. Yachts and boats can be hired with or without a crew, and there is no problem finding an agent who will arrange a day trip for those with no experience of sailing. Excursions off the peninsula by road, on the other hand, begin with an hour-long drive to the main coast road. If you are touring, a two-night stay should be sufficient, although the peninsula has plenty to offer by way of sandy beaches, accommodation and restaurants for a lazy couple of weeks.

✚ K16 🚌 Buses from Fethiye, İzmir, Kuşadası, Marmaris and Pamukkale
🛈 Bariş Meydanı 48 ☎ 0252 316 1091 🕐 Summer daily 8:30–7; winter Mon–Fri 8:30–12, 1–5:30

a walk around Bodrum

Walk from the tourist office with the sea on your left until you reach a Y-junction after a few hundred metres/yards. Bear right, passing the minaret of a mosque on the right, and walk up Cevat Sakir Caddesi. Walk past the post office on the left and then turn left, immediately before the otogar (bus station), on to Mumtaz Gorgün Caddesi. Turn left at Turgutreis Caddesi and continue along here until you reach the ancient mausoleum on the left.

The Mausoleum looks nothing like it did in the glory days of the 3rd century BC when it was classed as one of the Seven Wonders of the Ancient World.

After visiting the Mausoleum, start back along Turgutreis Caddesi, but turn right almost immediately down Haman Sok to reach the Bodrum waterfront for a walk by the water's edge along Neyzen Tevfik Caddesi to the marina.

After strolling past the magnificent yachts and gin palaces, browse the boutiques of the smart Marina Shopping Mall and maybe stop for a coffe, beer or glass of *raki*. There are lots of restaurants facing the sea here, so take time to read the menus .

Distance 5km (3 miles)
Time 2–3 hours
Start point Tourist office (➤ 131)
End point Marina
Lunch At one of the many seafront restaurants (➤ 143–145)

Bodrum Kalesi (Castle of St Peter)
Best places to see, ➤ 38–39.

Mausoleion (Mausoleum)
King Mausolus ruled ancient Caria for the Persians as a semi-independent state, and his love of Greek culture reached its zenith in the splendid tomb – the first 'mausoleum' – erected after his death in 351BC. It was one of the Seven Wonders of the Ancient World, but the Knights of St John demolished it and used its materials to build their castle. The massive foundations remain, but little else – assorted column pieces, parts of the outer wall and the underground vault. The site is still worth a visit, as an informative exhibition with models gives some flesh to the meagre remains. There are also plaster copies and a few original pieces of the so-called Amazon reliefs that were mostly shipped off to join other hijacked treasures in the British Museum in London.

✉ Turgutreis Caddesi ⏰ Daily 8–5
✋ Moderate 🍴 None nearby

Tiyatro (Theatre)
To the northwest of the mausoleum, the ancient theatre has been completely restored. It was started by King Mausolus, extensively adapted by the Romans, and is now used to stage events during the town's autumn festival. The view is somewhat marred by the noise from the main road.

🚌 *Dolmuş*/minibus

More to see around Bodrum

BEACHES

The nearest beach on the Bodrum peninsula itself is Gümbet, 3km (2 miles) away and easily reached by *dolmuş*, or on foot when the temperature drops (take the road inland after passing the marina). Gümbet, overdeveloped with package hotels, is the preserve of 18- to 30-year-olds. Further west is a mediocre beach at the more upmarket Bitez, and a better one at Ortakent (which is popular with Turkish families on holiday). Kagı, Bağla, Karaincir and Akyarlar, on the south coast of the peninsula, are quieter locations but have watersports (equipment for hire), and the sea is cleaner here than it is at the beaches nearer Bodrum.

✚ K16 🍴 Restaurants and beach cafés (£–££) 🚌 *Dolmuş*/minibus/boat from Bodrum

GÖKOVA KÖRFEZİ (GULF OF GÖKOVA)

There are boats and yachts for hire and agents to arrange day trips along Dr Alim Bey Caddesi near the tourist office, and at the main marina, off Neyzen Tevfik Caddesi. A typical itinerary visits Karaada (Black Island), which has hot springs and mud baths, before continuing to Ortakent beach (➤ 138) and skirting the Greek island of Kos (Turkish Istanköy) for a swim and lunch. Boats returning to Bodrum often pause at a shallow stretch of water christened 'the Aquarium' because of the marine life that can be seen.

Bodrum is the most popular departure point for a 'turquoise cruise' or 'blue voyage' along the beautiful 56km (35-mile) coastline of the Gulf of Gökova.

Gülets, the traditional broad-beamed wooden vessels of the area, can be chartered with a crew, and watersports equipment is usually included. Destinations include Yedi Adalar, a quiet bay on the southeast corner of the gulf, and Sideyri Adası (Cedar Island, ➤ 174), with the beach that Mark Anthony is supposed to have created for Cleopatra.

🚌 L16 ✉ Between Bodrum and Marmaris 🖐 Expensive 🚌 Boats and yachts from Bodrum and Marmaris

GÜMBET

This beach, the closest one to Bodrum, has become a self-contained resort, and is very popular with young people on two-week package holidays. There are hotels, pubs, nightclubs and restaurants in abundance; the 600m-long (650yd) beach is not superb, but even so you cannot be sure of finding a space in high summer. The best thing about Gümbet is the range of water-based sports and activities available on the beach.

✚ K16 ✉ 2km (1.2 miles) west of Bodrum 🍴 Restaurants (£–££)
🚌 *Dolmuş*/minibus from Bodrum

GÜMÜŞLÜK

A photogenic fishing village, half an hour's drive from Bodrum, Gümüşlük has been overrun by tourism. It's on the site of ancient Myndos and this has resulted in restrictions being imposed on new buildings. The fish restaurants along the waterfront are not inexpensive but they make a delightful stop. The 1km-long (half-mile) beach is a mixture of sand and gravel, and swimming in the sea at the south end brings you close to some Myndos ruins.

✚ J16 ✉ 15km (9 miles) west of Bodrum 🍴 Fish restaurants (££–£££)
🚌 *Dolmuş*/minibus from Bodrum

ORTAKENT

One of the better beaches on the Bodrum peninsula, Ortakent's sand stretches for 2km (1.2 miles). The road is closed to traffic, so it is a safe place for children. There is nothing to see or do here but enjoy the sun, sand and sea. Various watersports are available, but windsurfing is as fast as it gets here. Ortakent has become popular on a small scale with British package groups.

➕ K16 ✉ 10km (6 miles) west of Bodrum 🍴 Restaurants (£–££)
🚌 *Dolmuş*/minibus to Bodrum

TURGUTREIS

Turgutreis is totally dedicated to tourism, and package-holiday hotels abound. There are well over 100 restaurants, and a sufficient number of bars and nightclubs to keep visitors amused for a week or longer. The parasol-peppered beach has coarse sand and, because the sea remains shallow for quite some way out, it is suitable for young children.

➕ K16 ✉ 20km (12 miles) west of Bodrum 🍴 Restaurants (£–££) 🚌 *Dolmuş*/minibus from Bodrum

YALIKAVAK

Tucked away on the northern shore, this is one of the less developed of the many resorts on the Bodrum peninsula. The small town is pretty, in a manicured kind of way, with a restored 300-year-old windmill in the middle of a pedestrianized area of cobbled streets. There are far better beaches on the peninsula than Yalıkavak's pebbly one, and this helps to keep the crowds away (choose a hotel with a pool if you are staying here). Yalıkavak is ideal for people who want the facilities of bigger resorts, but not the non-stop nightlife.

➕ K15 ✉ 18km (11 miles) west of Bodrum 🍴 Restaurants (£–££) 🚌 *Dolmuş*/minibus from Marmaris

a round trip from Bodrum

Catch the morning car ferry from Bodrum to Körmen. The tourist office has ferry departure times. From here it is a 10-minute drive across the peninsula to the town of Datça (➤ 152).

On the way to Datça, a signposted road on the right leads west to Knidos (➤ 162–163) at the end of the peninsula. The road is not a good one, however, so unless you cannot wait to get there by boat, carry straight on here to Datça.

Turn left to take the main road (400) to Marmaris (about one hour's drive).

Marmaris (➤ 166–169) is the best place to stop for lunch.

From Marmaris, follow the signs inland to Muğla.

Beehives are dotted about in the surrounding forest: this is where the renowned pine-scented honey of Marmaris comes from.

About 15km (9 miles) after passing a right turn to Fethiye, turn off the main road, following signs to Muğla.

Alexander the Great marched his army through this mountain pass, but your vehicle will make the journey in far less time.

There are fine views of the Gulf of Gökova, with space to park and take in the scenery.

From Muğla (▶ 172), follow signs to Yatağan, which will bring you back to the main Bodrum road. At Yatağan follow signs for Milas (▶ 169) and from there turn south for Bodrum.

Distance 185km (115 miles)
Time 3–5 hours; full day if you decide to visit Knidos to swim
Start/end point Bodrum ✚ K16
Lunch Plenty of choice in town (£–££)

HOTELS

BODRUM
Karia Princess (£££)
This award-winning hotel is the classiest place to stay in Bodrum. It is a little way to the west of the town centre and consequently not plagued by disco music all night long. There is, however, a neat little cinema nearby and the largest supermarket to be found in any of the resort towns along the coast. The hotel's Turkish bath is a superb recreation of an Ottoman-style *hamam*. Most rooms have a pleasant balcony, and those that don't are less expensive.

✉ Canli Dere Sokak 15 ☎ 0252 316 8971; www.kariaprincess.com

The Marmara Bodrum (£££)
A beautiful contemporary boutique hotel set on a hillside overlooking Bodrum town, the castle and the bay. Rooms are spacious, chic and minimalist in style, and there's an excellent restaurant and spa on site. The views from the freeform pool are excellent.

✉ Yokubaşı Mah, Suluhasan Caddesi 18 ☎ 0252 313 8130; www.themarmarahotels.com

Queen Apartments (£)
A small complex of apartments, Queen epitomizes Turkish accommodation at the budget end of the price scale with simply furnished but clean rooms with kitchenettes in a low-rise block. There's a pool, bar and restaurant on site and it's just 200m (220yds) from the beach.

✉ Gündönümü Mevkii, Halilim Caddesi 3, Bitez ☎ 0252 363 9016; www.queenapart.com

Su Hotel (£–££)
There are at present ten air-conditioned rooms here, although there are plans for expansion. Cheerful decor greets you, along with a pool, bar, and fruit trees all around. It's a pretty cool place to stay.

✉ Turgutreis ☎ 0252 316 6906; www.suhotel.net

RESTAURANTS

BİTEZ

Daphne Restaurant and Bar (£–££)

The spacious verdant garden is a major draw of this restaurant, making al-fresco dining a pleasure. The menu mixes Turkish staples with pasta and the chef has been poached from the 5-star Hilton hotel in Izmir. There's live music every night year-round and in winter there's a roaring log fire warming the dining room, so it's a draw out of season too.

✉ Gözütok Sok 4 ☎ 0252 363 7722 🕓 Lunch and dinner

BODRUM

Antique Theatre Restaurant (£££)

Situated opposite the ancient theatre, this is one of the most prestigious restaurants in Bodrum. Seafood is a speciality, but international dishes such as duck with caramelized oranges, feature on the menu. Torch-lit poolside setting, with illuminated views of the Castle of St Peter at night.

✉ Kibris Sehitlehri Caddesi ☎ 0252 316 6053 🕓 Dinner only in summer
🚌 *Dolmuş*/minibus to Bodrum

Kocadon (£££)

This is the way one would like all of Bodrum to look; the restaurant is set among ancient-looking stone walls and houses enclosing a quiet courtyard with a small pool in a garden. Sparkling white linen on the tables, jazz or classical music in the background, and good Turkish cuisine add to the air of romance. Make a reservation and arrive in time to enjoy a cocktail by the poolside and soak up the atmosphere.

✉ Saray Sok 1 ☎ 0252 316 3705 🕓 Daily 8pm–midnight
🚌 *Dolmuş*/minibus to Bodrum

Kortan Restaurant (££)

One of the most established restaurants in Bodrum town and occupying a very central position with views across to the castle, Kortan offers a more upmarket atmosphere than many of its neighbours. The seafood here is excellent and includes interesting local options such as octopus casserole. The terrace is spacious and the dining room a lovely stone walled area.

✉ Cumhiriyet Caddesi 32 ☎ 0252 316 1300 🕓 Lunch and dinner

🚌 *Dolmuş*/minibus to Bodrum

La Jolla Bistro (££)

Full to bursting with eager drinkers in summer, out of season this is a delightful little wine bar, sushi bar and bistro on the seafront, with mouthwatering French-style cuisine, an extensive wine list and good cocktails. There's also a branch in the Xuma Beach Club, Yalıkavak from June to September.

✉ Neyzin Tevfik Caddesi 174, Karada Marina Karşısı ☎ 0252 313 7660

🕓 Lunch and dinner 🚌 *Dolmuş*/minibus to Bodrum

Marina Yacht Club (££)

There's more than one restaurant in this well-run complex, with live music every night. Locals like this place and with good reason: it's got a laid-back atmosphere, good seafood and friendly staff.

✉ Neyzen Tevfik Caddesi ☎ 0252 316 1228 🕓 Lunch and dinner

🚌 *Dolmuş*/minibus to Bodrum

Nur (££)

An elegant Mediterranean setting is successfully evoked in the courtyard of this town house. The menu is not large and the portions not huge, but there is a good selection of fish and meat dishes, and the atmosphere of the place compensates.

✉ Cumhiriyet Caddesi, Eski Adilye Sokak 5 ☎ 0252 313 1065 🕓 Lunch and dinner 🚌 *Dolmuş*/minibus to Bodrum

The Secret Garden (£££)

The food here is Mediterranean and includes frogs' legs in garlic, chicken and sage ravioli, seafood soup with vermouth, tomato and pesto tart and tapenade – and that's just the starters! Main dishes include slow-cooked lamb with aubergine, filet steak with spinach and rosti, sea bass and olive potatoes – you get the picture. It's basically some of the best food to be found on the Turkish west coast.

✉ Eskicesme Mah Danaci Sokak 20 ☎ 0252 313 1641 ⊕ Dinner only, summer only 🚌 *Dolmuş*/minibus to Bodrum

Tuti (£££)

The coolest and probably the most expensive restaurant in Bodrum, Tuti offers contemporary Turkish and European cuisine in a stylish setting. However, it's the views from the terrace across Bodrum that make a visit special, particularly in the evening as the sun sets. Splash out and enjoy the ambience and the refined service.

✉ The Marmara Bodrum Hotel, Yokusbaşı Mah, Suluhasan Caddesi 18 ☎ 0252 313 8130 ⊕ Dinner only 🚌 *Dolmuş*/minibus to Bodrum

GÖLTÜRKBÜKÜ
Mey (£££)

One of the favourites with the yachting crowd and with wealthy Turks. The *meze* are delicious, as is the seafood – but choose the seafood and the bill does get pretty impressive. There are fixed-price menus for those who would rather know what they are likely to spend. Reservations recommended.

✉ Atatürk Caddesi, Yalı Mevkii ☎ 0252 377 5188 ⊕ Daily lunch and dinner May–Oct

GÜMÜŞLÜK
Gümüş Café (££)

Situated at the quieter end of the beach, this is a restaurant where you can drop in at breakfast or lunchtime for delicious home-made bread, or enjoy an evening casserole – it's all in a lovely romantic setting.

✉ Gümüşluk ☎ 0252 394 4234 ⊕ Daily 8am–late May–Oct

Gusta (££)

A stylish addition to the eateries of the Bodrum peninsula – the contemporary Caribbean-style decor and modern menu make it bang up to date. The large terrace is great for a relaxed cocktail or a meal, and it's a terrific venue for people-watching.

✉ Yalı Mevkii ☎ 0252 394 3045 ⊕ Lunch and dinner

YALIKAVAK
Ali Baba (££)

Overlooking the harbour, this is an ideal spot to enjoy home-made *meze*, fish and steaks. *Pide* bread is cooked in a traditional oven.

✉ Seafront ☎ 0252 385 3194 🕒 Lunch and dinner 🚌 *Dolmuş*/minibus to/from Bodrum

SHOPPING

BODRUM
Bodrum Marina Shopping Centre

A small but elegant mall with upmarket shops and chic cafés that cater for the yachting crowds. Tommy Hilfiger, Nautica and Diesel have a presence here, though these are the genuine article (not the copies found in the bazaars) so prices are expensive.

✉ Neyzen Tevfik Caddesi ☎ 0252 316 1860 🕒 Shops: daily 10–9

Carpets and *kilims*

Heaps of carpets and above-average expertise in the person of Sayın Burku, whose workers have produced the world's largest Turish carpet (8.7m x 19.2m/ 29ft x 63ft) for a Kuwaiti sheikh.

✉ Neyzen Tevfik Caddesi 40 ☎ 0252 316 4571; www.sayinburku.com 🕒 Daily 9am–10pm

Dalyancı

One of the better shops for gifts, craft and souvenirs with pieces by local artist Engin Dalyancı. Glass and ceramics in a variety of designs and colours, with fixed prices.

✉ Cumhuriyet Caddesi, Alim Bey Pasaji 55 ☎ 0252 313 0214; www.dalyanci.com 🕒 Daily 8:30am–late

Dr Alim Bey Caddesi

Facing the tourist office, turn to the left, with the mosque on your right, and enter the pedestrianized Dr Alim Bey Caddesi. The street is full of shops selling leather, clothes, jewellery, shoes and souvenirs. The street eventually reaches the Halikarnas Disco, where the shops are replaced by bars and restaurants.

✉ Dr Alim Bey Caddesi 🕒 Daily 8:30–late

Gallery Mustafa

One of the better carpet and *kilim* shops in Bodrum. If your purchase is too big to carry to your hotel, the shop can arrange safe delivery to your home.

✉ Dr Alim Ekinici Caddesi 48 ☎ 0252 313 1043; www.gallerymustafa.com
🕐 Daily 9am–10pm

Gazelle Leather and Gift Shop Handicraft

There's a small collection of leather jackets and belts and a host of less expensive craft items, such as small inlaid boxes. There are also picture frames, a jewellery section, souvenirs and gifts.

✉ Neyzen Tefvik Caddesi 124 ☎ 0252 316 9707 🕐 Daily 9:30am–midnight

Oasis

The Bodrum peninsula's largest mall offers over 200 shops, with some good high-street fashion at competitive prices. It includes a children's play area, shady spots for relaxation, a food court, cafés, multi-screen cinema complex and a variety of entertainment venues.

✉ Emin Anter Bulvarı, Kibris Sehitleru Caddesi ☎ 0252 317 0002;
www.oasisbodrum.com 🕐 Shops: daily 10am–10pm

ENTERTAINMENT

BODRUM

Bodrum is heaving with bars and clubs. Dr Alim Bey Kok and Cumhuriyet Meydanı together make up the local 'bar street'.

Bodrum Marina Yacht Club and Bar

There's live music here every night with a mixture of classical jazz and Filipino tribute bands playing anything from The Beatles to Abba. It attracts a wide variety of age groups and nationalities, but is particularly popular with the more mature crowd.

✉ Neyzen Tefvik Caddesi ☎ 0252 316 1228; www.marinayachtclub.com
🕐 Daily 9pm–1am

Halikarnas Disco

This legendary outdoor disco is the number one hot-spot in Bodrum. The laser-and-light show, usually around midnight, is spectacular and there are exotic-looking belly dancers and leather-clad professional dancing groups. The DJs are very good.

✉ Cumhuriyet Caddesi ☎ 0252 316 8000; www.halikarnas.com.tr ◷ Daily 8pm–early morning

Marine Club Catamaran

This very large indoor disco is one of Bodrum's top nightspots. The light shows are worth catching. The DJs keep the rock music going and maintain a very upbeat atmosphere.

✉ Dr Alim Bey Caddesi, 1025 Sok 44 ☎ 0252 313 3600; www.clubcatamaran.com ◷ Daily 7pm–4am

Ora

A cavernous, ancient-looking building that usually manages to fill every inch of its floor space with revellers, this is one of the most popular bars in Bodrum. While the slogan of 'the bar where you can dance on the tables' is not always taken literally, it gives a good idea of the atmosphere.

✉ Dr Alim Bey Caddesi 19/21 ☎ 0252 316 3906 ◷ Mid-morning to late

'Quick Drink Street'

This is the literal translation of Tektekçiler Sokak, a narrow street filled with small wooden chairs and the sound of Turkish music played on traditional instruments. The idea is that one passes through this street, stopping for ten minutes or so to enjoy a drink and take in the music and singing, then moving on to somewhere else. The street is first right after passing the Ora pub.

✉ Tektekçiler Sokak ◷ Early–late evening

Southern Aegean

Turkey's southern Aegean coast has experienced tourism on a large scale for far longer than the north. Bodrum is the undoubted capital, but Marmaris, a little further south, is a worthy runner up.

Fethiye

Sitting at the head of its own rocky peninsula, Marmaris marks the most southerly point of the Aegean. The coast begins to turn west, and is known as the 'Turquoise Coast' because of the opaque sky-blue and green-blue colours of the Mediterranean that lap the shores.

The small town of Fethiye is an attractive base for a sun, sea and sand holiday, but it is also within easy reach of several fascinating historical sites, such as Kaunos and Knidos, dating back to the ancient kingdom of Lycia which once included this corner of the coast.

ALTİNKUM

'Lazy by day, lively by night' is one travel brochure's catchphrase for this popular package-holiday destination. The 1km (0.5-mile) beach is popular, especially with British visitors, though the whole area is a building site as developers fling up huge Costa del Sol type estates. There are tourist restaurants and a modern shopping centre specializing in goods such as watches and designer-label clothes. Of more enduring value, the superb Temple of Apollo at Didim (Didyma; ➤ 152–153) is just five minutes' drive up the road.

✚ K15 ✉ 5km (3 miles) south of Didyma 🍴 Tourist restaurants (£–££) 🚌 *Dolmuş/* minibus from Kuşadası

CALIŞ

This is the nearest beach, albeit a shingle one, to Fethiye, and the two places are linked by regular public transport by road and sea. The beach stretches for 2km (1.2 miles), and runs parallel to the road, which is closed to traffic in the high season. There is the usual array of hotels, bars and restaurants, but on the whole Calış is a lot quieter and more pleasant than nearby Hisarönü (➤ 157).

✚ P17 ✉ 5km (3 miles) north of Fethiye 🍴 Restaurants (£–££)
🚌 *Dolmuş/*minibus or ferry *dolmuş* from Fethiye

DALYAN

Dalyan is close to an airport and the main coast road, with Marmaris to the west and the sites of ancient Lycia to the east. Boats leave the quayside every morning before 10 to make the 40-minute journey to the ancient site of Kaunos (➤ 161) and

İztuzu beach, which is excellent for swimming as well as being a nesting site of the loggerhead turtle between May and October. Development has been prohibited here because the young turtles seem to be confused by bright lights. You can spend a day at İztuzu and return at half-hourly intervals in the afternoon. The beach has little shade, so take hats and suncream.

Another popular excursion is a ten-minute boat ride upriver to the thermal baths at Ilıca. A wallow in the open-air mud pools, which reach a temperature of 40°C (104°F), is said to do the body a power of good. In cooler months it is pleasant to rent a bicycle in Dalyan and cycle to Kaunos.

➕ N16 ✉ 13km (8 miles) south of the main Muğla–Fethiye road 🍴 Restaurants (£–££) 🚌 *Dolmuş*/minibus to Marmaris, Muğla and Fethiye ❓ Day tours from Dalyan combine İztuzu beach, Kaunos and Köyceğiz

DATÇA

This town, centrally located along the long and narrow peninsula that stretches west from Marmaris, has most of its shops and facilities laid out along one long main street. The harbour is attracting a growing number of yachts, and the town is slowly developing services for tourists: hotels, restaurants and bars with music are dotted along the seafront. Boat trips go to ancient Knidos and to various swimming places away from the town itself. The best place for swimming close to town is at the far side of the west beach.

🚌 L17 ✉ 75km (46.5 miles) west of Marmaris 🍴 Restaurants (£–££)
🚍 *Dolmuş*/minibus from Marmaris and Muğla, car ferry from Körmen, 9km (5.5 miles) north, to Bodrum (➤ 129–134)
ℹ In centre ☎ 0252 712 3163

DİDİM (DIDYMA)

This stupendous Temple of Apollo, built to house an oracle, should not be missed. The Persians destroyed one temple here in the late fifth century BC, and the one that now looms dramatically by the side of the road was begun about 300BC. A British archaeologist in the 19th century described the remains as 'piled up like shattered icebergs', but excellent restoration work has revealed the temple's mighty proportions and splendour. Be sure to walk to the back of the structure where one of the fallen columns has been preserved by archaeologists to show how it tumbled apart after falling. At the site entrance is an imposing head of Medusa, once part of a richly decorated frieze.

Steps lead up to the main platform and its 12 columns, and from here two tunnels lead down to the cellar. At the far side stood a small building where the cult statue resided. Here, next to the oracular spring, the prophetess delivered her utterances to the temple priests, who wrote them down and presented them to the client. Some fragments of the inscribed prophecies have been

found, but it is likely that most were destroyed by Christians who built a church inside the temple itself. The Romans built a stadium so close to the south that the bottom steps on this side of the temple were used as seats. Many names, carved on the seats to reserve places, can still be clearly made out. After visiting the temple, have a drink on the veranda of the Oracle *pansiyon* directly overlooking the west side of the site.

🕂 J15 ✉ 75km (46.5 miles) south of Kuşadası ☎ No phone 🕓 Daily 8:30–5:30 ✋ Inexpensive 🍴 Two restaurants (£) opposite site entrance 🚌 *Dolmuş*/minibus from Söke ❓ Tours from Kuşadası combine Miletus, Priene and Didyma

EUROMOS

The only substantial remnant of the ancient city of Euromos is its Temple of Zeus, but its setting among olive groves is so picturesque and the remains so evocative that it is well worth making the short detour if you are travelling between Milas and Kuşadası. Euromos was founded in the sixth century BC, and the temple owes its existence to the patronage of the Romans, probably Emperor Hadrian (AD117–38). The city itself was built 0.5km (0.3 miles) to the northwest of the temple, but there is little to see.

➕ L15 ✉ Between Lake Bafa and Milas, 2km (1.2 miles) southeast of Selimiye ◷ 24 hours. Ticket office has irregular hours but generally 9–12, 1–5 💷 Inexpensive 🚌 *Dolmuş*/minibus from Milas

FETHİYE

The modern town of Fethiye, occupying the site of ancient Telmessos, was completely rebuilt after a devastating earthquake in 1957, and the modern quayside and promenade stand on the rubble of the old city. There had been an earlier earthquake in 1857, so very little is left of ancient Telmessos.

Nothing is known about its origins, but it became part of Lycia, fell to Alexander in due course and was later ruled by Rome. Apart from the Lycian rock tombs (➤ 52–53) and an excavated Roman theatre near the tourist office (both easily taken in on an early morning walk through town, ➤ 158–159), the best reminder of ancient Telmessos is next to the post office in the centre of town. Here sits a large, double-fronted sarcophagus with an

arched lid, bearing fading reliefs of Lycian warriors. At the end of the 19th century it stood in the sea, but the fall of the sea level has returned it to dry land.

Although Fethiye is clearly a resort town, it is quite different from Bodrum or Marmaris. Less sophisticated, it has managed to avoid intense commercialism, retaining a recognizably Turkish character.

Like Bodrum and Marmaris, however, it has a quayside that bustles with activity each morning as tourists take their seats for one of the popular boat excursions to nearby beaches and islands. It also has plenty of restaurants and hotels for visitors, lively bars,

a Turkish bath (► 63), and lovely golden sandy beaches in the vicinity. Fethiye also makes a good base for visiting a number of major and minor ancient sites, or for an excursion to the ghost town of Kayaköy (► 162).

There is a small **museum** in the centre of town with some interesting archaeological finds from Letoön and Patara. The main bus station is 2km (1.2 miles) to the east of the town, and a *dolmuş* station, in the centre of town behind the mosque, serves the local beaches. The bus company, 'Pamukkale', also has offices in the centre of town, so it is relatively straightforward to book long-distance bus journeys.

Ölüdeniz (► 46–47) is, justifiably, the most popular and famous of the local beaches, but there are others nearby at Calış and Hisarönü. There are 12 islands dotting Fethiye Bay, and boat trips visit some of these for swimming and exploring.

➕ P17 ✉ 170km (105 miles) east of Marmaris, 80km (50 miles) northwest of Kalkan

ℹ️ Near harbour, İskele Karşısı 1 ☎ 0252 614 1527

Museum

🕐 Tue–Sun 8–5 🍴 Restaurants (£–££) 🚌 Bus to Denizli, İzmir, Kalkan, Marmaris, Pamukkale, Patara and Xanthos

HİSARÖNÜ AND OVACIK

Hisarönü and Ovacık are close to the coast, though not actually on it, and are busily developing as accommodation centres for the Fethiye region. Hisarönü, the larger and more popular of the two resorts, is very much a tourist satellite settlement for Ölüdeniz, 4km (2.5 miles) away down the hillside. Fish-and-chip shops testify to Hisarönü's popularity with the British; for a quieter destination, nearby Calış (► 150) is preferable. New bars and restaurants are opening in both Hisarönü and Ovacık, with a better choice of fare than the eating places on the beaches.

➕ P17 ✉ 10km (6 miles) south of Fethiye 🍴 Bars and restaurants (£–££) 🚌 *Dolmuş*/minibus from Fethiye

a walk around Fethiye

This walk starts at the tourist office at İskele Karşısı where you can collect a town map. After leaving the tourist office, turn right.

After 100m (110yds) you will pass the town's Roman theatre on the right (▶ 154). At the roundabout just ahead, take the inland street, by following the blue sign for Sokak 45.

You will soon pass a Turkish bath (▶ 63) and the Car Cemetery pub (▶ 184), one of the most popular in town, opposite each other. At the end of the street have a look in the Ottoman Café (▶ 185).

Turn left, then go down to the T-junction with the Atatürk statue and turn to the right, crossing to the other side of the street.

Just before the PTT (post office), a Lycian sarcophagus can be seen on the left (▶ 154).

Stay on the main road until you reach a gleaming mosque and at this junction turn right and walk up the cobbled street. At the T-junction, go left and cross to the other side. After a few hundred metres, turn right at a yellow sign for Kayaköy. Turn right at the top, and then left at the playground to walk up through houses to the site entrance for the Lycian rock tombs (▶ 52–53). To continue the walk, retrace your steps to the junction by

the mosque and carry straight across and down Hastane Caddesi, towards the sea, and have lunch in the hotel at the end of the street.

Distance 5km (3 miles)
Time 2–3 hours
Start point Tourist office ✉ İskele Karşısı 1
End point Yacht Plaza Hotel on the waterfront
Lunch Carpe Diem ✉ Ece Marina ☎ 0252 614 3986

IASOS

Populated from around 2000BC, ancient Iasos prospered under the Romans, and in Byzantine times the Knights of St John built a castle here. The last vestiges of the town lie by the side of the village of Kıyıkışlacık, whose name translates as 'the little barracks on the coast'. Most of what can still be seen belongs to the second century AD, including the remains of a Roman mausoleum and a *bouleuterion* (meeting hall), but it takes something of a leap of the imagination to picture them in their complete state. The Byzantine castle is the most impressive sight and gives fine views. A small museum stands over the mausoleum, and its fragmented exhibits found on the site are poignant reminders of the almost-vanished town.

✚ K15 ✉ Kıyıkışlacık, 8km (5 miles) northwest of Milas, 4km (2.5 miles) southeast of Euromos ⏰ Tue–Sun 8:30–12, 1–5 💲 Inexpensive 🍴 Fish restaurants (£) in Kıyıkışlacık 🚌 *Dolmuş*/minibus from Milas or boat from Güllük

KALKAN

Coming from Fethiye, the road suddenly reaches the top of a cliff and looks down to a little town hugging the cliffs in the curve of a bay. A well-kept secret among seasoned budget travellers and the yachting crowds until tourism made its impact in the early 1980s, Kalkan is growing rapidly, but is still a pleasant and more sophisticated alternative to Fethiye as a base for exploring this corner of the coast. The town centre's picturesque houses seem precariously attached to the hillside and there are steep cobbled streets, a pebble-beached cove, a good range of accommodation and decent restaurants.

✚ Q18 ✉ 80km (50 miles) east of Fethiye 🍴 Restaurants (£–££) 🚌 *Dolmuş*/minibus from Fethiye and Kas

KAUNOS

Ancient Kaunos was founded in the ninth century BC, and its ruins make a worthwhile excursion by boat from nearby Dalyan. Originally a Carian city, Kaunos came under the cultural influence of neighbouring Lycia, and this is apparent in its decorated rock tombs, which resemble the Lycian tombs at Fethiye (➤ 52–53). Archaeological work is still going on at Kaunos; the ruins include well-preserved sections of wall from the fourth century BC, and a theatre which was built some 200 years later. The most ornate of these tombs are carved into the sheer cliffs which have been worn over the years by the river so it's not possible to get up close to them.

In ancient times the Mediterranean came right up to the acropolis, but the marshland that now attracts mosquitoes (bring repellent) must have been in evidence in the past: Herodotus noted that the inhabitants were reputed to have yellowish skin, probably caused by malaria.

✚ N16 ✉ Dalyan (➤ 150–151) ☻ Daily 8:30–5:30 ✋ Inexpensive
🚌 Dolmuş/minibus from Marmaris, Muğla and Fethiye or boat from Dalyan
❓ Day tours from Dalyan

KAYAKÖY

This town of some 2,000 homes, once called Levissi, lost its Greek Orthodox inhabitants in 1923 in the exchange of populations that followed the War of Independence. The Turkish population left the settlement to the elements until its haunting beauty and fascinating history began to draw the first tourists in the 1980s. Now a UNESCO World Heritage Site, it is being restored as an historic village. So far it has a few *pensiyons* and wine bars. Louis de Bernière based his book *Birds Without Wings* on it.

✚ P17 ✉ 7km (4 miles) south of Fethiye
🕐 24 hours. Ticket office has irregular hours but generally 9–1, 2–5 ✋ Inexpensive
🍴 Restaurants and cafés (£) 🚌 *Dolmuş/* minibus from Fethiye

KNİDOS

The location is an appealing one – the exposed tip of the spiny Marmaris peninsula – and the ancient city of Cnidus was built here to benefit the Mediterranean sea trade. The settlement grew rich and famous, and at one time its proudest inhabitant was a statue of Aphrodite, carved by Praxiteles, the Michelangelo of the time. The statue has disappeared but there are various remnants of the old city, spread over a wide area: the most substantial are the Hellenistic theatre and the Byzantine basilicas, and you can also see the remains of a lighthouse and necropolis. The view is spellbinding, with a number of Greek islands – Ródos (Rhodes), Kos (Cos), Giali (Yiali), Níssyros (Nisiros) and Chálki (Khalki) – visible from the ruins. A rough road leads to Knidos (➤ 140), but it is much more pleasant to take a boat from Datça. Day-long boat trips include stops for lunch and a swim.

✠ K17 ✉ 35km (22 miles) west of Datça
🕓 Daily 8–7 ✋ Inexpensive 🍴 Fish restaurants (£–££) near dock 🚌 Boat from Datça or Mamaris

KÖYCEĞİZ

A peaceful inland town on Köyceğiz Gölü (Lake Köyceğiz), without the intense commercialism of coastal resorts, Köyceğiz has a modest appeal. The lake is the centre of attraction and there are regular boat excursions to the opposite shore, where you can bathe in the life-enhancing mud of the Sultaniye Kaplıcaları. These thermal baths, rich in calcium, potassium and sulphur, attract far fewer visitors than those at Ilıca and also benefit from a more interesting setting. Boats also cross the lake to Dalyan and Kaunos: ask at the tourist office in the main square for details.

✠ N16 ✉ 50km (31 miles) east of the Muğla–Marmaris road 🍴 Restaurants (£–££)
🚌 *Dolmuş*/minibus from Marmaris and Muğla
ℹ️ Main square ☎ 0252 262 4703 🕓 Mon–Fri 8:30–12:30

LABRANDA

The Sanctuary of Zeus at Labranda is not easy to reach, even with your own car, but the effort is richly rewarded. A few kilometres outside Milas, on the main road heading north to Selçuk, the turn-off is signposted on the right. The site is 14km (9 miles) further on, and the paved road ends after 6km (4 miles) at the village of Karigeak. It is not advisable to try the drive in winter unless it is very dry. Swedish archaeologists have done some work here at Labranda, and the main ruins are clearly marked. The most interesting are the two structures where devotees held their sacrificial banquets, and an impressive fourth century BC tomb. The isolated setting and the sweeping views afforded by the steep location of these little-visited ruins make this one of the more evocative ancient sites of the Turkish Aegean.

✚ L15 ✉ 17km (10.5 miles) north of Milas 🕐 Daily 8:30–5 ✋ Inexpensive
🚌 Car or taxi from Milas

LETOÖN

Letoön, the Lycian centre for the worship of Leto, was an important sanctuary in ancient times. First excavated in 1962, the remains of three third century BC temples, dedicated to Leto, Artemis and Apollo, bear testimony to its significance. Leto was a nymph who was loved by Zeus, and was jealously hounded by his wife Hera as a consequence. Wolves guided the pregnant Leto to the River Xanthos, where she bathed and renamed the place Lycia (from the Greek for wolf, *lykos*) before giving birth to Artemis and Apollo.

Alexander the Great came here and received encouragement for his imminent battle against the Persians. There is also a Hellenistic theatre and an inscription found here was instrumental in the eventual deciphering of the Lycian language.

✚ Q18 ✉ Kumluova, 6km (4 miles) southwest of Xanthos 🕐 Daily 8:30–5 ✋ Inexpensive 🚌 *Dolmuş*/minibus from Fethiye to Kumluova

MARMARİS

Set by the side of an 8km-long (5-mile) bay and framed by pine forests and oleander shrubs, Marmaris looks out to sea where the Aegean and the Mediterranean meet. The town's name is said to come from a remark by Süleyman the Magnificent in 1522 – *mimari* translates as 'hang the architect'. He was unimpressed by the fortress he was using for an attack on the Knights of St John at Rhodes. In 1798, the British Admiral Nelson used the bay to prepare his fleet for an attack on the French at Abukir.

Along with Kuşadası and Bodrum, Marmaris is one of the big three coastal resorts on the Turkish Aegean, and manages to satisfy most modern visitors. There is a strong contingent of young people who are here to party and, as in Kuşadası, one of the roads has become known as Bar Street. Families come here on package holidays, which often include free accommodation for children, and many of the hotels have a children's pool and play area. Marmaris also has a very large and modern marina with a highly affluent clientele, hence the expensive restaurants around

town. Other visitors find that neighbouring İçmeler, now virtually a suburb, is ideal as an accommodation base, while still being handy for shopping in Marmaris' bazaar and sightseeing in the area.

Marmaris may lack Bodrum's air of sophistication, but a stroll along the promenade at dusk does have its charms. Islands and coves can be made out in the bay, scores of brightly painted boats nod at their moorings, and chains of twinkling lights enhance the scene. Restaurants, bars and cafés line the pedestrianized road and tempt you to take a seat under the palm trees.

The statue of Atatürk near the waterfront is the hub of the town centre. The statue divides the two main streets that face the harbour, Atatürk Caddesi to the west and Kordon Caddesi to the east. The main inland road that comes down to meet the statue is Ulusal Egemenlik Bulvarı. Most places of interest are to the east of the statue, and Kordon Caddesi leads to the tourist office, banks, post office and shops.

There is a small **museum** behind the tourist office, and a tiny castle sits like a crown at the very top of the town, but most

visitors prefer to check out the shops or organize day trips to the nearby islands of Rhodes, Kaunos or Knidos and numerous other destinations, either by sea or by land.

✚ M16 ✉ 170km (105 miles) west of Fethiye, 165km (102 miles) east of Bodrum 🍴 Restaurants (£–£££) 🚍 Buses from Bodrum, Fethiye, İzmir and Pamukkale

🛈 İskele Meydanı ☎ 0252 412 1035 🕓 Summer daily 8:30–7; winter Mon–Fri 8:30–12, 1–5

Museum

🕓 Daily 8–12, 1–5 👌 Inexpensive

MİLAS

This agricultural town and centre of carpet production was the site of ancient Mylasa and capital of the Carian kingdom. Follow the main street, Kadıağa Caddesi, which becomes Gümüşkesen Caddesi, to reach the large Roman tomb known as the Gümüşkesen, about 1km (0.5 miles) west of the town centre. It may be a copy on a smaller scale of the Mausoleum of Halicarnassus (Bodrum,

➤ 134). Retrace your route to the very beginning of Kadıağa Caddesi, on the east side of town near the canal, where there is an attractive 14th-century mosque, the Ulu Cami. Take the road north from here for about 250m (270yds), and the Baltalı Kapı will come into view. Known as the Gate with an Axe, this Roman gate has a double-headed axe carved into a stone on the north side.

✚ L15 ✉ 45km (30 miles) northeast of Bodrum 🍴 Restaurants (£) 🚍 Buses from Marmaris and Kuşadası

🛈 Milas–Bodrum Airport ☎ 0252 523 0101

a drive from Marmaris to Pamukkale

Leave Marmaris, following signs for Muğla.

About 12km (7.5 miles) after passing the right turn for Fethiye, the road climbs through a mountain pass to reach Muğla (➤ 172), and there are splendid views of the Gulf of Gökova (➤ 136).

As you approach the ring road at Muğla, follow signs to Denizli.

The road (330) to Denizli is over 100km (62 miles) along a scenic route, which is very much off the beaten tourist track. The changing colours of the landscape as the road weaves its way towards the village of Kale are enchanting.

From Kale the road continues to Tavas. Turn left if you want to make a diversion (60km/37 miles return) to Afrodisias (➤ 78). If not, follow the Afyon/Ankara road out of Denizli and after about 8km (5 miles) take the left turn, signposted to Pamukkale.

Very soon after this turning, just before the village of Korucuk, there is a left turn signposted to Laodikeiá. Save this visit for later and press on to Pamukkale (➤ 48–49). This is the best place for lunch, after which you can explore Hierapolis (➤ 44–45).

In the evening, if time allows, it does not take long to drive down to Laodikeiá. If you turn left onto the main road in the direction of Ankara, it is less than 2km (1.2 miles) to a crumbling old caravanserai on the left side of the road as you reach the bottom of a hill.

Distance 150km (93 miles), excluding Aphrodisias
Time 4–5 hours
Start point Marmaris ✚ M16
End point Pamukkale ✚ P13
Lunch Anatolia Restaurant, Afrodisias

MUĞLA

Start by calling at the tourist office and collecting a town map; this is a town to walk around at a leisurely pace, taking in the general air of prosperity.

The most interesting area to explore is the old Ottoman quarter, with its winding streets of pretty buildings. From the tourist office by the Atatürk statue, head north up Kurşunlu Caddesi and take a look in at Yağcıar Hanı, a modern shopping centre in a converted caravanserai. The street continues north up to the town's bazaar, also worth visiting, and higher up on the hillside are many photogenic houses. These are well-preserved examples of domestic Ottoman architecture.

✚ M15 ✉ 73km (45 miles) north of Marmaris ❚❚ Restaurants (£) in the centre of town 🚌 *Dolmuş*/minibus to Bodrum, Denizli, İzmir and Marmaris
🛈 Emirbeyazıt Mah ☎ 0252 214 1261; www.mugla-turizm.gov.tr
🕐 Mon–Fri 8–7, summer; Mon–Fri 8–12, 1–5, winter

ÖLÜDENİZ

Best places to see, ➤ 46–47.

ÖREN

It is easy to miss Ören: after leaving Milas and travelling south for 3km (2 miles), look for the main junction where the road goes right for Bodrum. Turn left instead for Muğla; the turn for Ören is very soon after on the right. Ören is a pleasant coastal village, used more by Turkish families than foreign holidaymakers, with an attractive 1km (0.5-mile) pebbly beach, and the scant remains of the ancient city of Ceramus. Public transport is infrequent, and it is best to drive yourself. The **Byzantine fortress** here is a good place for a picnic, although you will have to pay to get in.

L16 ⊠ 55km (34 miles) south of Milas ⋔ Restaurants (£) near beach
🚍 Occasional *dolmuş*/minibus from Milas

Byzantine fortress
🕐 Daily 8am–dusk ✋ Inexpensive

PATARA

A very wide 18km (11-mile) sandy beach is the great attraction of Patara; a conservation area for birds and turtles, so the beach closes at dusk. Be cautious when swimming: there are some strong currents and no shade, so go prepared. The ruins of ancient

Patara, an important supply base for the Romans, are 1km (0.5 miles) away. It was once a port, but was engulfed by sand. The highlight is undoubtedly the sand-filled theatre.

✚ Q18 ⊠ 7km (4 miles) south of Xanthos 🕐 Summer daily 8–8; winter daily 8:30–5 (site)
✋ Inexpensive (ancient site)
⋔ Restaurants (£) on beach
🚍 *Dolmuş*/minibus to Fethiye and Kalkan

PINARA

This is not an easy to place to reach, even with your own transport, but the journey is attractive, and lets you indulge in the illusion that you have just discovered ancient Pınara yourself. Very little is known about the place, except that it was an important Lycian city that minted its own coins. The most compelling spectacle is the openings cut into in the huge mass of rock that towers over the site. They are thought to be tombs, but access is impossible to all but dedicated rockclimbers and should not be attempted. There are other tombs at ground level and the most interesting of these, the Royal Tomb, displays fine reliefs showing people and walled settlements. Of the other ruins, the theatre is the best preserved. Bus travellers have to walk the last 5km (3 miles) from the Pınara turning.

➕ Q17 ✉ 46km (28.5 miles) southeast of Fethiye 🕐 Open 24 hours ✋ Inexpensive 🍴 Snacks (£), 2km (1.2 miles) 🚌 *Dolmuş*/minibus from Fethiye to Pınara turning

ROCK TOMBS, FETHIYE

Best places to see, ➤ 52–53.

SİDEYRİ ADASI (CEDAR ISLAND)

Legend has it that Mark Anthony had all the fine sand on the beach brought from northern Africa as a personal gift to the Egyptian queen: hence the name Cleopatra's Beach. The beach is the main attraction for the many people who visit on day trips from Marmaris and Bodrum. Tours from Marmaris include road transport to the boat at Çamli İskelesı. The island's name comes from the ancient city of Cedrae. It was sacked by the Spartans during the fifth century BC Peloponnesian War, and retained its Greek culture until Arab invasions in the seventh century AD.

➕ M16 ✉ Gulf of Gökova 🚌 Boats from Taşbükü and Çamli İskelesı ❓ Tours from Marmaris include road transport to Çamli İskelesı

SİDYMA

This is the least visited of the Lycian sites because there is no public transport. What can be seen mostly dates back to Roman times, although there are some Lycian rock-cut tombs, a pillar tomb that has lost its grave-chamber from the top and an interesting row of sarcophagi. The site is always open.

✚ P17 ✉ South of Eşen 🖐 Free

TLOS

Ancient Tlos was one of the more important Lycian cities, and in the 19th century it became a winter headquarters for a pirate called Kanli Ali Ağa. The ruins reflect this mixed parentage. The empty remains of the pirate's fortress tower over the site from the top of the acropolis, and the Lycian remains include excellent examples of rock-cut tombs. The theatre is in good condition, but the baths are the most interesting of the other

scattered remains. During 2007, an archaeological team started a research programme at the site and certain areas may be off limits to visitors during the dig.

🞤 Q17 ✉ 48km (30 miles) north of Xanthos at village of Kale Asar
🕐 24 hours 👋 Inexpensive 🚌 No public transport

TURUNC

Turunc used to be a place to escape from the crowds of Marmaris. Tourist brochures still portray the modern resort as a relaxing hideaway, but this is stretching the truth. The 500m (545yd) beach of coarse sand, with a splendid backdrop of cliffs and pine trees, is the focus of daily activity. It is safe for swimming and you can hire watersports equipment. Water taxis bob next to the jetties, waiting to take people to coves along the coast.

🞤 M16 ✉ 10km (6 miles) south of Marmaris 🍴 Restaurants (£–££)
🚌 Dolmuş/minibus from water dolmuş to Marmaris

XANTHOS

From the modern village of Kınık, on the main Fethiye–Kalkan road, it is a five-minute walk to the ancient Lycian capital of Xanthos and its Harpy Tomb (➤ 54–55). The acropolis overlooks the Eşen Çayi River, and it is easy to imagine the Lycians looking down on the plain in the sixth century BC as a Persian army advanced on their citadel. Rather than surrender, they set fire to their city, and those who did not die fighting perished in the flames. The ruins of the new city that arose in the fifth century BC are now the major attraction. In 42BC the Roman general Brutus attacked the city, only to be confronted by another act of mass suicide as the Lycians realized that defeat was imminent. Under Roman rule the city thrived again, and in Byzantine times it was a centre of Christianity. A path leads to the remains of a Byzantine church, a pleasant lunch spot.

✚ Q18 ✉ Just north of Kınık, 63km (39 miles) from Fethiye
🕐 Nov–Apr daily 7:30–7; May–Oct daily 8–5:30 👢 Moderate 🍴 Café (£) 🚌 *Dolmuş*/minibus from Fethiye or Kalkan

XANTHOS, HARPY TOMB

Best places to see, ➤ 54–55.

HOTELS

DATÇA
Dede Pansiyon (£)

Some 3km (2 miles) from Datça, this *pansiyon* is about six rooms with kitchen in a stone dwelling in a lovely rustic setting. It's a great place to stay when the day tours have left and you have the place to yourself. Check out the 1950s fridge by the poolside bar.

✉ Eski Datça ☎ 0256 712 3951; www.dedepansiyon.com

DALAMAN
Pegasos Tropical (£££)

A large 500-room luxury all-inclusive resort hotel with beautiful modern Turkish styling and a full range of on-site activities. The huge central free-form swimming pool is the most stunning feature. It's situated close to the airport at Dalaman on a good stretch of beach.

✉ Sarigerme, Ortaca ☎ 0252 286 8510; www.joyhotels.com

İÇMELER
Aqua (£££)

Pleasantly landscaped, with palm trees and a garden leading down to the beach. The amenities of İçmeler are within walking distance. The 240 rooms have balconies with partial sea views. Suitable for families; adults can use the fitness centre, gym and tennis court.

✉ İçmeler ☎ 0252 455 3633 ▣ *Dolmuş*/minibus from/to Marmaris

KALKAN
Kalkan Regency Hotel (££)

This modern multi-level hotel is set above the coastline around the pool like a traditional Turkish village around it's square and offers panoramic views. There's a lovely sitting room with games and a small library, though you are much more likely to want to soak in the sun on the deck.

✉ Kalamar Yölü, Kalkan ☎ 0242 844 2230; www.kalkan.com.tr/regency
🕒 May–Oct

KAYAKÖY
Villa Rhapsody (£)
This small hotel in the Kaya Valley, close to Kayaköy, offers peace and quiet. There are walking routes to nearby hills and farms and to Kayaköy. The villa is surrounded by gardens where you'll find the swimming pool with pool bar, and there's a restaurant on site.

✉ Kayaköy ☎ 0252 618 0042; www.villarhapsody.com

MARMARİS
Begonya (£)
A cut above the average mid-range hotel in the middle of Marmaris, this is a stone-built house with its own courtyard and characterful architecture. Nearby pubs can be noisy.

✉ Hacı Mustafa Sokak 101 ☎ 0252 412 4095

Kaya Maris (££)
This 256-room tourist hotel is just 50m (55yds) from the beach and a half-hour walk from central Marmaris. There is a main pool and a children's pool, Turkish bath, gym, sauna and watersports.

✉ Kenan Evren Bulvarı ☎ 0252 413 0233; www.hotelkayamaris.com
🚌 Dolmuş/minibus to/from Marmaris

ÖLÜDENİZ
Meri (££)
This is the place to soak up the sun at Ölüdeniz, and the only hotel inside the designated national park area. There are 75 rooms, a restaurant and garden bar, a playground area for children and laundry. All the usual water-based activities can be arranged here, including diving. Lift service to the beach.

✉ Ölüdeniz ☎ 0252 617 0001; www.hotelmeri.com 🚌 Dolmuş/minibus to Fethiye

Montana Pine Resort (£££)
Set among the forests above Ölüdeniz, with stunning lagoon views, the resort has spacious rooms with balconies, restaurants, bars, a health club and three pools. Shuttle bus to the beach.

✉ Ölüdeniz ☎ 0252 616 7108/6366; www.montanapine.com 🕐 Apr–Oct

RESTAURANTS

FETHİYE

Marina Lokantası (££)

Formerly known as Rafet, this is one of Fethiye's oldest and best restaurants, specializing in seafood, perfectly sited on the promenade by the fishing harbour.

✉ Kordon Boyu ☎ 0252 614 1106 🕔 Lunch and dinner

Meğri (£)

A well-established restaurant that has acquired a good reputation for its authentic Turkish meals. To order, just point to the dish you want. There is a second Meğri restaurant in Çarşı Caddesi.

✉ Eski Cami Gecidi Likya Sokak 8 ☎ 0252 614 4047 🕔 Lunch and dinner

İÇMELER

Kerem (££)

A traditional Turkish menu is offered here, featuring favourites such as steamed lamb shin and kebabs. What adds to the pleasure of dining here is the style of the building, designed by a famous architect – ask the owners for details.

✉ Osmangazi 24 ☎ 0252 455 4869 🕔 Lunch and dinner

MARMARİS

Antique Café (££)

The location, on the first-floor balcony of the Nestel Marina, gives the Antique an edge over restaurants with lesser views. The food is excellent; great salads.

✉ Nestel Marina ☎ 0252 413 2955 🕔 Daily 8am–late

Pineapple (££)

Another restaurant in the Nestel Marina, this one is on the ground floor, and residents of Marmaris rate it as one of the best half dozen in the town. International cuisine, in a pastoral setting.

✉ Nestel Marina ☎ 0252 412 0976 🕔 Daily 8am–midnight

Portofino (££)
Recommended for its choice of Turkish and British food at
reasonable prices. It's a family-orientated, friendly establishment,
but beware that it does have satellite sports on a large-screen TV.
✉ Cildir Mah Sokak 164 ☎ 0252 413 2261 ◷ Daily 8:30am–late

ÖLÜDENİZ
Beyaz Yunus (White Dolphin) (£££)
With a fabulous setting overlooking the eastern end of Ölüdeniz
beach, a Mediterranean garden and superb food, including
seafood specials, this is the place to go for a celebratory night out,
or just to enjoy the best this area has to offer.
✉ Ölüdeniz beach ☎ 0252 617 0068 ◷ Lunch and dinner May–Oct
🚌 Dolmuş/minibus from Fethiye

Levissi Garden Wine House and Restaurant (££)
This renovated stone cottage with a lovely garden in the ghost
village serves memorable meals and some reasonable house
wine, with stews, roasts and summer barbecues. The perfect
place for a relaxing lunch or pleasant dinner.
✉ Gökçeburun Mahallesi 70, Keçiler ☎ 0252 618 0108 ◷ Lunch and dinner
🚌 Dolmuş/minibus from Fethiye

Restaurant La Turquoise (££)
A poolside restaurant for the Montana Pine Resort Hotel, which
serves international cuisine. The pleasant setting and the live
classical Turkish music contribute to the ambience of fine dining
at a reasonable price.
✉ Montana Pine Resort, Ölüdeniz ☎ 0252 616 6366 ◷ Lunch and dinner
🚌 Dolmuş/minibus from Fethiye

SHOPPING

DİDYMA
Gallery Kirşehir
An onyx factory and shop, directly opposite the temple of Apollo,
with vases, jars, ashtrays and other assorted items for sale.
Potential customers are shown around the factory.

✉ Harabeler Kar, Didyma ☎ 0256 811 0306 🕐 Daily 8am–9pm
🚌 *Dolmuş*/minibus from Söke

FETHİYE
Erol's Gold
Precious and semi-precious stones and the whole range of rings, necklaces, bracelets and wonderful earrings. Prices are negotiable and the company has an excellent reputation.
✉ Hisarönü, Fethiye ☎ 0252 616 7496 🕐 Daily 9am–10pm

Old Orient *Kilim* Bazaar
Two floors of hand-made carpets and *kilims* from all over Turkey. Run by a friendly, soft-sell proprietor who repairs carpets when the tourist season ends. Some souvenirs for sale also.
✉ Karagözler Caddesi 5, Fethiye ☎ 0252 612 1059 🕐 Daily 9am–midnight

MARMARİS
Duygu Bag Shop
A bazaar shop with quality leather travel bags, hand bags, belts and briefcases. There are marked prices on the items but you can still ask for a discount.
✉ Kenan Evran Bulvarı, Istaklal Caddesi 9, İçmeler, Marmaris ☎ 0252 455 4030 🕐 Daily 9am–midnight

Nur-Bal
A jar or two of Marmaris honey make a distinctive local souvenir, and this little shop, in the block behind the post office, has a good selection. The dark-coloured, black-pine honey is one of the local specialities, and the *portakal* is a light-coloured and very sweet variation.
✉ Tepe Mah, Yeniyol Caddesi, Marmaris ☎ 0252 412 3731 🕐 Daily 8:30am–10pm

Oriental
A self-styled 'carpet palace', this comfortable shop is easy to find, just next to the tourist office facing the sea. It has a reasonable selection of carpets and *kilims*, but you should go knowing

something about what you want and the likely price – as in all such stores, the prices are not exactly the same for all customers. Some astute bargaining would not go amiss here.

✉ Yat Limanı 3, Marmaris ☎ 0252 412 4818 ⊕ Daily 8am–midnight

Ottoman

Silver jewellery, clocks, pocket watches, copper utensils, hand embroidery and other items – part of the pleasure of this shop is its chaotic-looking arrangement. It is a serious shop, though, with genuine antiques, and shipping can be arranged. Inland, near the bazaar.

✉ Çeşme Mey Grand Pazar 1, Marmaris ☎ 0252 412 5911 ⊕ Daily 9am–10pm

Vogue Jewellery & Diamond Centre

What it says on the tin, a large emporium glistening with gold and precious stones, plus jewellery made to your own design. They offer a hotel shuttle and will even bring things to your hotel room!

✉ Kemal Elgin Bulvarı, Marmaris ☎ 0252 6 413 4875; www.voguediamond.co.uk ⊕ Daily 9am–10pm

ENTERTAINMENT

FETHİYE
Car Cemetery Pub

This well-known establishment has a pool table upstairs, cappuccinos and toasted marshmallows early in the evening and cocktails and iced chocolate later. There are more pubs in the immediate vicinity, but the Car Cemetery is always worth a visit.

✉ Karagözler Caddesi, Fethiye ☎ 0252 614 2521 ⊕ Daily 4pm–late

Ottoman Café

It is a little surprising there aren't more pubs like this one along the coast. The interior recreates an Ottoman-style atmosphere with the help of antique copper pots adorning the walls and Turkish folk music. It's sometimes taken over by package groups, but it can make a relaxing venue during the afternoon.

✉ Karagözler Caddesi 3/B, Fethiye ☎ 0252 612 1148 ⊕ Daily 10am–4pm

HISARÖNÜ
Grand Boozey Bar
This is a no-frills bar with taped music and a snooker table that is popular with English visitors. The place never really goes over the top, but can be relied on to remain convivial and...well, boozy.
✉ Hisarönü ☎ 0252 616 6726 🕐 Daily 11am–late 🚌 *Dolmuş*/minibus to Fethiye

İÇELMER
Joy
This is a well-established disco in İçmeler and its circular shape makes it easy to identify. It's on the right side of the main road as you come into İçmeler from Marmaris.
✉ İçmeler ☎ 0252 455 3302 🕐 Daily 11pm–3am 🚌 *Dolmuş*/minibus to Marmaris

MARMARİS
Back Street Disco
A long-standing local favourite, this noisy club manages to maintain its popularity through a mix of brash sound and light, great food, a large dance floor, open-air terrace and cocktails.
✉ Bar Street, Marmaris ☎ 0252 412 4048; www.backstreetdisco.com 🕐 Until late 🚌 *Dolmuş*/minibus to Marmaris

ÖLÜDENİZ
Buzz Bar Beach
A great place for a beachside lunch or early dinner, but the bar really livens up after 10pm. The waterside setting is great, and the cocktails are amazing.
✉ Ölüdeniz ☎ 0252 617 0045; www.buzzbeachbar.com 🕐 Daily 10am–2am

Help Bar
On the beachfront promenade, Help has been a staple on the nightlife scene for a while and has lots of loyal fans. There's a long cocktail list and some great bar snack-style food.
✉ Ölüdeniz ☎ 0252 617 0498 🕐 Daily 10am–2am

Index

Acknowledgements

The Automobile Association would like to thank the following photographers, companies and picture libraries for their assistance in the preparation of this book.

Abbreviations for the picture credits are as follows – (t) top; (b) bottom; (c) centre; (l) left; (r) right; (AA) AA World Travel Library.

4l Castle, Bodrum, AA/J F Pin; 4c Bus, AA/ C Sawyer; 4r Ölüdeniz, AA/J F Pin; 5l Kadınlar Plaji, AA/P Kenward; 5c Kadifekale Castle, İzmir, AA/J F Pin; 6/7 8/9 Tiles on sale, AA/P Bennett; 10/11t Whirling Dervishes, Tourism Turkey; 10/11b Books for sale, AA/P Bennett; 10c Drinking fountain, AA/P Bennett; 10b Local women, AA/P Bennett; 11t Ruins at Knidos, AA/P Kenward; 11c Local with pony, AA/P Bennett; 12/13t Restaurant, Gümüşlük, AA/J F Pin; 12c Sesame simits display, AA/P Bennett; 12bl Sorting raisins, AA/P Bennett; 12br Turkish food, AA/P Bennett 13 Vendor AA/P Bennett; 14 Carving a kebab, AA/P Bennett; 14/15 Lemons on sale, AA/P Bennett; 15tl Turkish delight, AA/P Bennett; 15tr Turkish tea, AA/P Bennett; 16/17 Stadium, Ephesus, AA/J F Pin; 16 Cemerberlitas baths, AA/P Kenward; 17 Backgammon, AA/T Souter; 18/19 Çannakale Strait, AA/J F Pin; 19tl Cruise boat, AA/J F Pin; 19tr Divers, AA/J F Pin; 20/21 Bus, AA/C Sawyer; 24 Atatürk and Youth May festival, Christopher Furlong/Getty Images; 27 Jeep, AA/P Bennett; 28 Bus line, AA/J F Pin; 31 Pay telephone, AA/P Bennett; 32/33 Turkish police officers, AA/P Bennett; 34/35 Ölüdeniz, AA/J F Pin; 36 Artefacts at Afrodisias, AA/P Bennett; 36/37 Ruins, Afrodisias, AA/D Miterdiri; 37 Artefacts, Afrodisias, AA/P Bennett; 38/39t Bodrum Castle, AA/J F Pin; 38/39b Bodrum Harbour, AA/J F Pin; 40/41t Çeşme by night, AA/J F Pin; 40/41b Çeşme mosque, AA/J F Pin; 42 Ruins at Ephesus, AA/D Miterdiri; 43 Tourists at Ephesus, AA/J F Pin; 44 Roman theatre, Hierapolis, AA/P Kenward; 44/45 Amphitheatre, Hierapolis, AA/P Bennett; 46 Lagoon at Ölüdeniz, AA/P Kenward; 47 Ölüdeniz, AA/P Bennett; 48 Travertine pool, Pamukkale, AA/P Bennett; 48/49 Swimmers, Pamukkale, AA/P Bennett; 50/51 Remains at Asklepeion, Pergamum, AA/P Bennett; 52/53 Pergamum, AA/J F Pin; 54/55t Ancient Xanthos, AA/P Bennett; 54/55b Amphitheatre, Xanthos, AA/P Bennett; 56/57 Kadinlar Plaji, AA/P Kenward; 58/59 Holidaymakers eating, AA/T Souter; 61 Cyclists, AA/C Sawyer; 63 Mud baths, AA/P Bennett; 64 Library of Celsus and Curetes Street, Ephesus, AA/P Bennett; 64/65 Temple of Serapis, Ephesus, AA/J F Pin; 65 Curetes Street, Ephesus; 66/67 Windsurfer, AA/J F Pin; 69 Turkish slippers for sale, AA/P Bennett; 70 View to Lesbos, AA/P Bennett; 72/73 Beach at Patara, AA/J F Pin; 74/75 Craftswoman, İzmir, AA/J F Pin; 77 Foça, AA/J F Pin; 78/79 Ruins at Alinda, A/P Kenward; 80 Ruins of Temple of Athena, Assos, AA/P Bennett; 80/81 Ruins of Temple of Athena, Assos, AA/P Bennett; 82 Ayvalik, AA/P Bennett; 83 Bozcaada Island fisherman, AA/J F Pin; 84/85 Quayside, Çanakkale, AA/J F Pin; 85 Fort, Çandarlı, AA/J F Pin; 86 Blue Tomb, Bursa, AA/P Kenward; 86/87 Tophane Park, Bursa, AA/P Kenward; 88/89 Dilek Peninsula, Kuşadası, © Images&Stories/Alamy; 90/91 Library of Celsus, status, Ephesus, AA/J F Pin; 92 Ephesus, AA/P Kenward; 93 Restaurant, Foça, AA/J F Pin; 94/95 Lone Pine Cemetery, Gallipoli, Photolibrary Group; 95 Turkish War Memorial, Gallipoli, AA/P Kenward; 96/97 İzmir, AA/P Kenward; 99 Ottoman Clock Tower, İzmir, AA/J F Pin; 100 Atatürk Statue, İzmir, AA/P Kenward; 100/101 Yali Mosque, İzmir, AA/P Kenward; 102 Kuşadası, AA/P Kenward; 103 Kadinlar Plaji, AA/P Kenward; 104/105 View over Kuşadası, AA/P Bennett; 106/107 Lake Bafa, AA/P Bennett; 107 Ruins on an island, Lake Bafa, AA/P Bennett; 109 Wall of Prayer, House of the Virgin Mary, Meryemana, © Carol Dixon/Alamy; 110 Mosque window, Miletus, AA/P Bennett; 110/111 Theatre, Miletus, AA/P Kenward; 112 Ruins of Temple of Apollo, AA/P Bennett; 112/113 Gymnasium ruins, Sardis, AA/P Bennett; 115 Sığacık, fortress, AA/J F Pin; 116 Theatre at Troy, © David Ball/Alamy; 117 Ramp to City Gate, Troy II, © Dennis Cox/Alamy; 118 Wooden Horse, Troy, AA/D Miterdiri; 129 Snorkeller, Gümüşlük, AA/J F Pin; 130 Fisherman, Bodrum, AA/P Kenward; 131 Harbour, Bodrum, AA/P Kenward; 132 Castle of St John, Bodrum, AA/P Kenward; 133 Marina, Bodrum, AA/P Bennett; 134/135 Black Fig Beach, Bodrum, AA/J F Pin; 136/137 Gümüşlük jetty, AA/J F Pin; 138/139 Ortakent, AA/J F Pin; 140/141 View over Bodrum, AA/J F Pin; 149 Baths at Ilica, AA/P Kenward; 150 Water sports, Caiş Beach, Fethiye, AA/J F Pin; 151Cliffs at Dalyan, AA/P Kenward; 152 Detail of the Furious Medusa, AA/P Bennett; 152/153t Temple of Apollo, Didyma, AA/J F Pin; 152/153b Sculpture of a Lion, Didyma, AA/P Kenward; 154/155 Fethiye, harbour, AA/P Kenward; 155 Street vendor, AA/P Kenward; 156 Quayside, Fethiye, AA/P Bennett; 158/159 Fethiye coastline at night, Photolibrary Group; 160/161 Kalkan, AA/P Kenward; 162/163 Knidos, AA/P Kenward; 164/165 Labranda, AA/D Miterdiri; 166/167 Marmaris, AA/J F Pin; 168 Ottoman Castle, Marmaris, AA/J F Pin; 169 Roman Mausoleum, Milas, AA/P Kenward; 170 Lycian Tombs, Kale, AA/J F Pin; 170/171 Pecin Kale Castle, AA/P Kenward; 171 Kale Harbour, AA/J F Pin; 172/173t Muğla, AA/P Kenward; 172/173b Amphitheatre, Patara, AA/P Bennett; 174/175 Greek theatre, Pınara, Photolibrary Group; 176/177 Lycian Rock Tombs, Tlos, AA/P Kenward; 176 Lycian fortress, Tlos, AA/P Kenward; Lycian Pillar Tombs, Xanthos, © Nik Wheeler/Alamy; 178b Amphitheatre ruins, Xanthos, © Jack Sullivan/Alamy

Sight Locator List

This index relates to the maps on the covers. We have given map references to the main sights in the book. Grid references in italics indicate sights featured on the town plans. Some sights within towns may not be plotted on the maps.

Dear Reader

Your comments, opinions and recommendations are very important to us. Please help us to improve our travel guides by taking a few minutes to complete this simple questionnaire.

You do not need a stamp (unless posted outside the UK). If you do not want to cut this page from your guide, then photocopy it or write your answers on a plain sheet of paper.

Send to: **The Editor, AA World Travel Guides,
FREEPOST SCE 4598, Basingstoke RG21 4GY.**

Your recommendations...

We always encourage readers' recommendations for restaurants, nightlife or shopping – if your recommendation is used in the next edition of the guide, we will send you a **FREE AA Guide** of your choice from this series. Please state below the establishment name, location and your reasons for recommending it.

_____
_____
_____
_____
_____

Please send me **AA Guide** _____

About this guide...

Which title did you buy?

AA _____

Where did you buy it?_____

When? m m / y y

Why did you choose this guide? _____
_____
_____
_____
_____

Did this guide meet your expectations?

Exceeded ☐   Met all ☐   Met most ☐   Fell below ☐

Were there any aspects of this guide that you particularly liked? _____
_____
_____
_____

continued on next page...

Is there anything we could have done better? _____
_____
_____
_____

About you...
Name (*Mr/Mrs/Ms*) _____
Address _____
_____
_____ Postcode _____

Daytime tel nos _____
Email _____ • _____

Please only give us your mobile phone number or email if you wish to hear from us about
other products and services from the AA and partners by text or mms, or email.

Which age group are you in?
Under 25 ☐   25–34 ☐   35–44 ☐   45–54 ☐   55–64 ☐   65+ ☐

How many trips do you make a year?
Less than one ☐   One ☐   Two ☐   Three or more ☐

Are you an AA member? Yes ☐   No ☐

About your trip...
When did you book? m m / y y   When did you travel? m m / y y

How long did you stay? _____

Was it for business or leisure? _____

Did you buy any other travel guides for your trip? _____

If yes, which ones? _____
_____
_____

Thank you for taking the time to complete this questionnaire. Please send it to us as soon as
possible, and remember, you do not need a stamp (*unless posted outside the UK*).

| **AA** Travel Insurance call 0800 072 4168 or visit www.theAA.com |